Mountain Biking the Coast Range
Guide 11

Orange County
and
Cleveland National Forest

by Robert Rasmussen

Edited by Réanne Douglass and Sue Irwin
Maps by Sue Irwin

FINE EDGE
Productions
BISHOP, CALIFORNIA

ACKNOWLEDGMENTS

I'd like first to thank my wife Jane and my daughter Anna. Not only did they understand the inscrutable, they were supportive of it. To my own friends, many thanks. Steve Koletty and Mike Murphy read manuscripts and commented. Bill Yarger and Brenda Siefford urged me on, as did several co-workers. I thank especially my secretary, Julie Schaller, who did much of the typing of the initial manuscript. (She found the subject interesting, although threatening to hair and nails.) Special thanks to BGR, South Orange County's oldest mountain biking club—unofficial, but continuous. The following rangers have been kind enough to give their time and comments to this text: Fran Calwell, USFS, a wealth of information and helpful spirit; Spencer Gilbert, State of California, gentleman and committed individual; Tom Maloney, County of Orange, Aliso and Woods Canyon Park; Stan Bengston, County of Orange, Caspers Park; Ranger Eaton, State of California, Crystal Cove State Park.

Important Disclaimer

Mountain biking is a potentially dangerous sport in which serious injury and death can and do occur. Trails have numerous natural and man-made hazards, and conditions may change constantly. Most of the routes in this book are not signed or patrolled. This book may contain errors and omissions and is not a substitute for proper instruction, experience and preparedness.

You must accept full and complete responsibility for yourself while bicycling. The authors, editors, publishers, land manager, distributors, retailers and others associated with this book are not responsible for errors or omissions and do not accept liability for any loss or damage incurred from using this book.

Introduction

Enjoying the land, delighting in the ride—these form the very essence of mountain biking. From Orange County's mountains to the sea you can find many types of riding. Opportunities for hard backcountry riding are everywhere. Leisurely tours of beautiful beaches and harbors are also found locally. Both the urban rider and backcountry enthusiast will find plenty of varied cycling. Examples:

River valleys. These canyons are oak-shaded with seasonal streams. They occur in the easy to moderate levels of difficulty, usually with modest elevation changes.

Rolling hills and meadowlands. After the first rains these areas are filled with wildflowers from late winter through spring. The variable ascents and descents of this terrain provide fast tracks for the mountain biker.

Mountain trails. Steep mountainsides rise hundreds of feet within short distances. These venues provide steep downhill runs — rock-strewn slaloms to delight the mountain biker.

Urban rides. The stability, durability, and comfort of the mountain bike makes it an ideal choice for traveling in town. Many fine trails exist throughout Orange County, enabling the urban rider to visit the county's most beautiful areas. Beaches and harbors are readily accessible through a series of interlocking trails. Mountain biking in urban Orange County is a delight not to be missed.

A Backcountry Experience

I began this project because I enjoy the wilderness and mountain biking. Very simply, this book is to introduce people to the rich and rugged terrain of Orange County, possibly some of the best urban terrain in the United States for the mountain biker. When riding, you experience the backcountry in little ways. You're aware of the plants and smells of the outdoors. Occasionally you see quail, deer, or roadrunners.

A Word on Navigation and Maps

I urge you to read the area descriptions well before using the trail maps. Your understanding of the terrain and how the maps relate to it will be greatly enhanced. Then use the book's maps as general guides, but do not rely on them for navigation. The Orange County Topographical Map (see page 96) and USGS 7.5 minute series of topographical maps are best. Pertinent topographical maps have been listed for each group of rides (or single rides as necessary).

Mountain Biking Seasons

The coastal canyons provide beautiful riding from November through May. But from June through October daytime temperatures can be extremely high. Riding in the early morning or early evening can help overcome this problem. But during these months you might consider higher elevations like the San Bernardino or San Gabriel mountain ranges (see page 96).

Area Map, Agencies and Riding Organizations

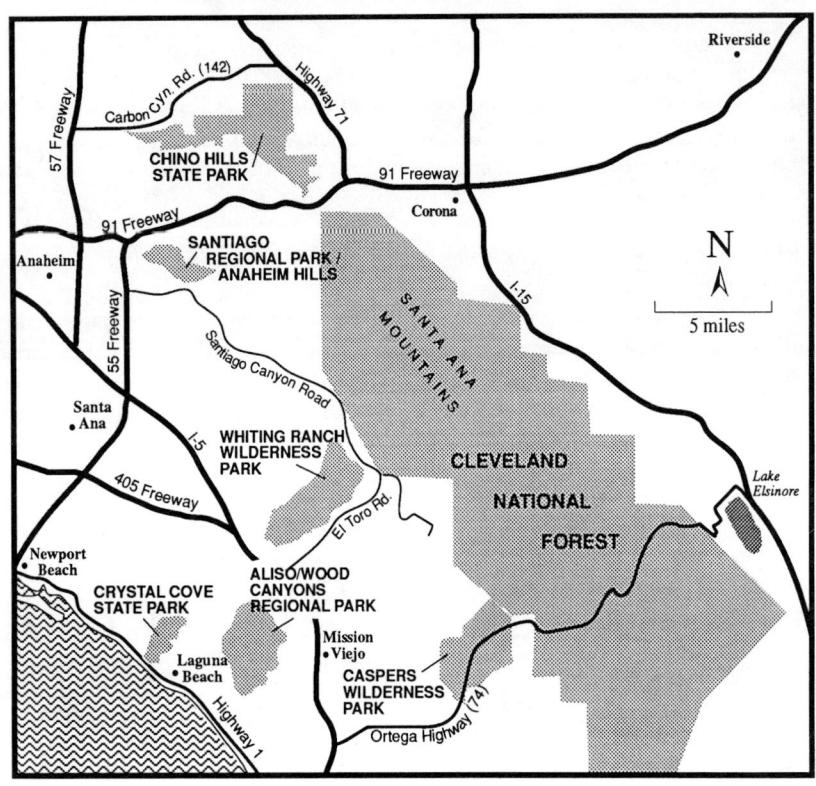

Agencies

Aliso/Wood Canyons Regional Park
(a division of Laguna Niguel Regional Park)
28241 La Paz Road
Laguna Niguel, CA 92667   (714) 831-2174

Chino Hills State Park
4195 Chino Hills Parkway #E165
Chino Hills, CA 91709
(No regular phone communications)

Cleveland National Forest/
Trabuco Ranger District
1147 E. 6th Street, Corona, CA 91719
Call for gate openings/closures–
Corona: (714) 736-1811
Silverado Fire Station: (714) 649-2645
(inconsistent office presence)

Whiting Ranch Wilderness Park
P.O. Box 156
Trabuco Canyon, CA   (714) 589-4729

Crystal Cove State Park (Moro Canyon)
8471 Pacific Coast Highway
Laguna Beach, CA 92651   (714) 494-3539

Santiago Oaks Wilderness Park
2145 Windes Drive
Orange, CA   (714) 538-4400

Riding Organizations

For questions and membership write:
"SHARE" – Bob Loeffler
3535 E. Coast Highway, #226
Corona Del Mar, CA 92625

Chino Hills Bicycle Assistance Unit
c/o Richard Cunningham (Mantis Bicycles)
(714) 993-4621

The author and publisher welcome information
regarding new **legal** trails on public land. Contact
Fine Edge Productions, Route 2, Box 303, Bishop,
CA 93514.

Table of Contents

Photo: Mickey McTigue

Historical Overview

Various Indian tribes inhabited Southern California in prehistoric times. The major aboriginal settlements were concentrated mostly on the coast where the rich ocean provided bountifully for the people. Inland Orange County was used sparingly by local tribes. Camps in our Santa Ana Mountains (Cleveland National Forest) were mostly seasonal, used for hunting and gathering purposes. As a reminder of that time, several early-man trails still exist there today. Santiago Truck Trail and San Juan Trail are two examples covered in this book. Both trails may be ridden deep into the mountains.

Often described as idyllic, the life-style of the local Indians ended abruptly in 1769, when Junipero Serra and his Spanish-Mexican soldiers founded the first California mission at San Diego. Labor was needed to build and staff these religious/economic enterprises. The Indians were impressed at gunpoint and marched from their villages to be relocated in mission housing. From fishermen and hunter-gatherers the locals became farmers, tradesmen, and ranchers. The mission kept a small military guard to maintain order. The new Spanish colonial society soon became permanent.

In 1776 a new country called the United States of America rebelled against the colonial excesses of its master, Britain. That same year Spain founded Mission San Juan Capistrano in what is today South Orange County. The pattern of development at Mission San Diego was repeated here, and the local Juaneño Indians were absorbed into the mission system.

For a time, California grew slowly. Its internal population didn't expand much and immigration was minimal. Politically and economically the new Spanish colony was isolated. Its food and farm products were a long way from markets. The colony was at the far end of a decrepit political system. No one in power thought much about *Alta California.* Consequently, through the years of Spanish and Mexican government, the people of California were left pretty much alone. They developed local leadership around the *hacendados* or powerful landowners such as Sepulveda, Pico, and Vallejo, families whose lives have been romanticized in literature and on film. (Zorro was a Hollywood *hacendado.*) These cattle barons ruled over their lands like princes.

After 1780 contact with foreign ships, especially American, became increasingly common. First it was whaling ships; then began the trade in cowhides. California was one vast cattle ranch. Neither Spain nor democratic Mexico ever developed thriving markets for California's goods — it was left to the young American republic to change the tide of events.

The steam engine was developed around 1780, and its power was soon harnessed to many tasks. New industries like the mass production of leather shoes began in Massachusetts and Connecticut. American ships poured into ports up and down California to buy and barter for cowhides. Indeed, early on so much trade was conducted with Boston that the "Californios" thought Boston was the U.S.

American author Richard Henry Dana in *Two Years Before the Mast* described his experiences in Southern California. His ship anchored off Dana Point (Orange County) in 1835 to take on leather cargo from local ranchers. Today a replica of Dana's ship, the *Pilgrim,* lies at anchor in Dana Point Harbor.

After the Mexican-American War and the California Gold Rush, the state grew rapidly. Orange County, originally part of Los Angeles County, split off as a separate entity, and its name became associated with the production of citrus products. All manner of ranching and agriculture bloomed in late 19th-century Orange County.

The place names of Orange County reflect its colorful history. Silverado Canyon was the site of numerous failed mining ventures in the Santa Ana Mountains. Trabuco Canyon was named after an 18th-century Spanish cavalry weapon, *trabuco:* one of these large caliber muskets was lost by a soldier there. Vulture Crags in early times was a nesting spot of California condors (it is now condorless).

The Santa Ana Mountains were an important watershed for coastal Orange County cities. By the late 19th century, destruction of habitat from timber cutting and brush fires began to threaten water supplies for lowland towns. The federal government created the Trabuco Canyon Forest Reserve in 1893 to improve environmental conditions. Fifteen years later an expanded Cleveland National Forest was founded, covering mountain areas in Orange, Riverside, and San Diego counties.

The government's management of the Santa Ana Mountains was "custodial" in the earliest days of the National Forest. This means the Feds wanted to protect and maintain the area in its natural state. Little development was planned, and modest numbers of trails and campgrounds were later added to develop the recreational aspects of the area.

Orange County now offers numerous mountain biking opportunities. Mountains, hills, valleys, harbors, and ocean views — it's all there in a relatively small area. The trips described herein may be enjoyed by Orange County residents within 30 to 60 minutes of their homes. Seriously, do you want to drive a long way after the week's commuting to have your fun? Discover and enjoy Orange County.

Special Considerations

Undoubtedly as you begin your riding adventures in the mountains, you will see other riders engaging in dangerous riding practices. We hope this book will help you along your way in developing not only good skills but also responsible manners. The code of behavior on the trail as detailed by the International Mountain Biking Association (IMBA) will make you part of the solution rather than part of the problem. See the "IMBA Rules of the Trail" in the Appendix of this book.

When riding at the many local parks of Orange County, complete outdoor preparedness doesn't seem like a priority. As you venture farther out into the mountains, however, this all changes. You must increase your level of awareness and preparation. You can find yourself a long way into the hills in a short time. Here are a few things to think about when attempting longer distance rides.

(1) **Water:** Water is found in many of the valleys of the Santa Ana Mountains. However, I never drink the stuff. Bring all the water you're going to need with you. Don't go out with less than two full bottles. If it's really hot, gallons of water may not be sufficient. (If it's that hot, maybe you shouldn't go out.) Force yourself to drink in warm conditions whether or not you feel thirsty.

Untreated drinking water can lead to severe conditions of diarrhea. Giardiasis, the most severe problem caused by bad drinking water, can make you very ill until you receive medical help. Don't drink any water without treating it first. The best method for the biker is to use water purification tablets, which are lightweight and efficient. (Water purifying mechanisms produce a superior-tasting product, but they are bulky and heavy compared to tablets.)

(2) **Courtesy:** Know and follow the IMBA Rules of the Trail. Extend courtesy to all other trail users by stopping to exchange greetings. (This lets others on the trail know you're aware of their presence and that you probably won't kill them.)

Get involved in supporting mountain biking. Contact local clubs that do trail work and that support responsible riding. Don't be a bad example for mountain bike riding. Be informed and responsible.

(3) **Preparedness:** Prepare a checklist for your trips before going out. Know your abilities, limitations, and equipment before the ride. You must have the proper amount of water, food, clothing, spare parts, and bike repair tools.

At the top of the list of essentials is a helmet. Wear one. The paths are full of rocks. I have plenty of nasty gashes in my helmet. Include also gloves and good eye wear. Layered clothing, adding and subtracting as necessary, is the way to go.

Riding alone in the backcountry has potential safety drawbacks. If you injure yourself, no one will know or come to help. If you can't find anyone to go out with you, then throttle back a bit. Very few people get hurt by going slower.

(4) **Conditions in the Mountains:** The higher you go into the mountains, the greater toll the sun takes on your body. Skin burns, lips dry out, and moisture is drawn out of the body. These severe conditions require the Orange County mountain biker to learn how to deal with dehydration, sunburn, heatstroke, and hypothermia. Read up on these first aid subjects.

Sluggish or cramped leg muscles show a need for calories. High energy foods like nuts, granolas, and dried fruits are just the thing to quickly replenish the body with powerful energy.

The sun in open mountain areas can damage your eyes, lips, and skin. Use a sunscreen with a rating of 15 or higher, and wear sunglasses with UV protection to guard against damage to the retina of the eye.

(5) **Horses:** You often see horses on Orange County trails. Some of them are easily spooked by mountain bikers. Therefore, it is the responsibility of the cyclist to take control of each encounter to ensure the safety of all.

If you see horses coming toward you, yield the right-of-way. Take your bike to the downhill side of the trail and well off it if possible. Quietly let the animals pass. If horses can see you well, they are less likely to get scared. A frightened animal can cause serious injury to riders, bystanders, and itself.

When approaching horses from behind, you must stop before passing. Get the attention and permission of the equestrians in front of you to pass. Then pass the horses on the downhill side of the trail (slowly and quietly).

(6) **Environmental Considerations:** There are many different ways to minimize your impact on backcountry areas.
• Leave plants, animals, historical sites and buildings alone and untouched.
• Stay on established trails and roads. Stay off private property. Follow posted Forest Service rules and use good sense in the absence of clear-cut instructions.
• Beware of seasonal fire closures. When in doubt, inquire at the local Forest Service office or park headquarters.

(7) **Safety Issues:** Control your bike. Guard against excessive speeds. It is neither fun nor healthy to crash. On steep downhill runs it is best to lower the seat of your bicycle. By lowering your center of gravity, you are less likely to launch yourself over the handlebars.

Keep your bike in good mechanical condition. The punishment of mountain riding shakes everything loose on the bike. Keep a high level of maintenance awareness, and this will help keep your machine from breaking down 10 miles out in the bush. Learn how to fix your bike. Bring a good repair kit with you and some spare parts (tubes, chain links, cable, etc.).

I question the usefulness of tire patching kits, however. When fixing leaks, one normally immerses the leaky tube into water to check for bubbles, the sign of a puncture. But in the Orange County backcountry there's almost no water. Better to bring a couple of extra tubes. Better still is to buy a product called "Mr. Tuffy." This product is a plastic insert placed between tube and tire. In a year of using these inserts, I've not lost a tube to thorns or sharp rocks. I still take along extra tubes, but my tire puncture problems have been cut to just about zero.

(8) **First Aid and Safety:** (See Appendix for a list of first aid supplies.) Carry your first aid kit. You will need it one day. Also, if you have allergies, bring along your medicine.

Injuries from crashes can be minimized by keeping your speed under control and slowing down in uncertain situations. Protective gear — helmets, gloves, over-the-ankle boots, long pants, and shirtsleeves — also goes a long way in minimizing injury. Good eye wear is a must.

In the Orange County backcountry there are certain things to be on the lookout for regarding the local residents:

Rattlesnakes are found throughout this area. You'll never see a snake until you're right up on it. They usually run quickly if given a chance. Snakes are often found hidden in rocks or brush. Stay on the trails and your chances of seeing a rattler are greatly reduced. Most often you'll see rattlesnakes in the months of April and May. That's when they come out of hibernation and they're not fully awake yet. (Otherwise they wouldn't let themselves get caught in the open.)

Tarantulas are other creatures you are quite likely to see, especially in August and September, their mating season, when they migrate in large numbers. The local variety of tarantula is essentially harmless; they can bite, but they cannot seriously hurt you. The diet of the tarantula is other insects, and they probably keep you from being eaten alive by the local insect population. Thus tarantulas are your furry and slightly horrifying-looking friends. Respect them accordingly.

Deerflies are a spring and summer annoyance in Orange County. There's nothing you can do about deerflies except to keep moving. As long as you're in motion, they can't get a fix on you. Stop and you're a buffet.

Ticks are everywhere in brushy country. Long sleeves and long pants are your best protection against ticks, and this clothing will also help you from getting cut up in the thick brush. The last line of defense against ticks is physical inspection before you leave for home. Check yourself out or have your friends do it and vice versa. Tick-related illnesses are on the rise.

Poison oak is a bush or vine that causes an unpleasant skin irritation. It is a three-fingered leaf, green or sometimes purple/red in color. It is often found near creeks or among oak trees. Staying on the trail usually keeps you from contacting poison oak. Avoid contact with not only the plant but with clothes or anything else that touched it. Immediately washing an affected area helps to lessen the effects of the plant.

(9) **Navigation and Trip Planning**: As mentioned earlier it's a good idea to know how to read topographic maps and how to use a compass. If you can do these two things, you'll probably know where you are in the mountains at all times. The maps in this book are in no way meant to replace topographical maps or their Forest Service counterparts. Another important thing to remember is that many trail numbers found on the Forest Service maps are not included on topo maps. Learn how to read these maps and bring both types with you.

Getting lost or breaking down is easy. Before leaving on a trip, tell someone where you'll be going and what to do if you don't return on time. If you're more than 6 hours overdue, have them contact the local County Sheriff. Give them the details about your vehicle and trip plans.

While traveling, keep track of your position on the map and write in the time when you arrive at a known position on the map. Look back frequently to get a sense of the way you came in case you have to go back that way.

Never be afraid to turn back. If conditions are deteriorating and it seems that your goals cannot be met safely, then it's time to turn around. Those who would jeopardize your safety by urging you forward are not your friends, and it would be best if you didn't ride with them any more. Safety first! The mountain will always be there tomorrow.

Laguna Canyon

From the ridges atop Moro Canyon you can see the area around Laguna Canyon. In a daring political and financial move, the city of Laguna Beach purchased a large chunk of this land from developers, attempting to save it in its natural state. This event has great potential significance for us mountain bikers. More land could be open to riding and our range of operation could be greatly increased. Get involved with your local mountain biking club. Write local and regional land managers. We need your help.

About These Rides

To find the best trip for you and make it as pleasant as possible I have rated these rides in the following ways:

Beginner, Easy: Usually flat terrain with little in the way of rocks and obstacles to bring a "Newbie" (new rider) to grief.

Intermediate, Moderate: These rides require more experience and stamina than beginner rides, and they may include steep climbs, relatively long distances, or some technical riding. However, they are not excessively dangerous or strenuous.

Difficult, Expert: These trails are often technical, with substantial elevation gains and long distances. A technical ride may include narrow, rocky trails or a steep drop at the side of the trail that requires expert bike handling. A dirt fire road is considered technical if it is rutted, rocky, steep, and fast.

Most of the riding in Orange County is done on fire roads that are often in rough shape (especially after rains). To take your eyes off the road for a second is to invite disaster. (I believe this is the essence of enjoyment in mountain biking. The ride requires your complete attention, and everything else on your mind is pushed aside.)

The single track available in Orange County is quite technical and best attempted after you've had some experience on your bike. After a few rides you'll get a good idea of what type of rider you are. Work your way up slowly. If you have friends you're training as potential partners, then have mercy on them. If you ask too much of them early on, they'll never want to go out with you again.

I rate myself as an intermediate rider. In these difficult mountain conditions I'm a firm believer of those concepts espoused in "The Tortoise and the Hare" — slow but steady.

CHAPTER 1

SANTA ANA MOUNTAINS / CLEVELAND NATIONAL FOREST
An Overview of Chapters 2-8

The early morning air is clear and cool. From the mountain a vast panorama unfolds. To the north, east, and south lie three major mountain ranges including four counties and a view encompassing hundreds of square miles. Where are we? The San Bernardinos, or perhaps the Sierras with their elaborate vistas? No, this is Santiago Peak, about 15 miles from Irvine—Orange County's equivalent to Silicon Valley.

At 5,687 feet Santiago Peak is the highest point in the Santa Anas, a mountain chain running north to south across eastern Orange County. A good portion of the Santa Ana Mountains lies within Cleveland National Forest, a rugged area of steep mountainsides and narrow, rocky valleys covered with thick vegetation. Though close to urban areas, Cleveland National Forest is a true backcountry area. The harshness of these mountains will convince you that travel would be impossible without the trails and roads that were so laboriously built here — the area would be totally inaccessible. Indeed, the region is even home to deer, wild cats and coyotes.

The one time I've ever seen a mountain lion in the wilds was in Orange County. It was a beautiful sight (from behind the refuge of my driver's side door!). When you think of how strong and agile the average house cat is and multiply that many times over to approximate the strength of a 100-pound mountain lion, it makes you glad that most of the time they fear humans.

The highest peak in the region: Santiago? Saddleback? Modjeska? The answer is Saddleback Mountain and all of the above. Most people in Orange County are thoroughly confused about this. Saddleback Mountain is actually made up of two separate peaks — Modjeska and Santiago — which are connected by a long ridge or saddle.

Water and Fluids

The Santa Ana Mountains are high and steep. From the high ridges where the majority of bike trails (fire roads) are located, mountainsides plunge 1,000 feet or more to the narrow river valleys below, which usually provide a water source in winter and spring. Do not drink the water, however, without adding purification tablets or filtering it. Many trails begin in these valleys and head up into the mountains. Water is not located where you'll need it, so don't venture into this area without a minimum of two quarts of water and even a third in warm weather. Also, if temperatures are high, you may want to consider carrying along electrolyte drinks or salt tablets (if you don't have any salt-related health problems). Your body will be severely depleted of fluids and chemicals in hot weather. These precautions will help you maintain your strength and vitality under tough conditions. November through April are the preferred months for bike travel in this area. May through October can be hellish, depending on how

Author Bob Rasmussen: Self-Portrait

you handle heat.

Trails beginning in river valleys are pleasant tree-shaded affairs. Generally speaking, traveling a few hundred feet up a switchback will take you into a sun-exposed area of chaparral where you'll remain the rest of the time. Steep switchbacks where you climb 2,000 to 4,000 feet in fully exposed sun are the norm in the Santa Ana Mountains. Because of these conditions, choose early morning or late afternoon to ride in this area during warm weather.

If I could think of one word to describe the riding conditions in the Santa Anas, that word would be "brutal." It takes everything you've got to ride *up* onto the Main Divide Truck Trail (3S04). Beginning riders don't belong here. Intermediate riders can adequately struggle their way to the top, and advanced riders should find the Santa Anas thoroughly challenging and enjoyable. Do not bring inadequately conditioned friends into the area.

Road Safety

Another aspect of the Main Divide Trail has to do with two- and four-wheel drive vehicles. There is a limited amount of traffic here, most of it occurring on weekends. When you encounter other vehicles, ride as far away from the road bed as you safely can. These roads are narrow, and you can easily lose control. Add to that the high probability of alcoholic drivers on weekends, and I'll gladly give the right-of-way to any approaching motor vehicle.

Gate Closures

The USFS closes backcountry gates after the first major rains of the season (usually December) and does not usually re-open them until May 1 This especially effects auto traffic in Silverado Canyon. It coincides neatly with the end of the best part of bike season. (Looks like you'll be getting up early to beat the heat if you want to make a car shuttle up on the high ridges.)

In Silverado Canyon I don't recommend taking a two-wheel drive vehicle any farther than the four-way trail junction of Maple Spring Road, Harding Truck Trail, North and South Main Divide. Conditions become increasingly treacherous beyond that point. Call the USFS office in Corona to confirm the status of the USFS gate.

Mountain Bikes and Trail Damage

I once belonged to a nature group that damned mountain bikes as destroyers of trails and roads. I routinely accepted this view until I rode a mountain bike and didn't notice any damage (except for trail cutting). Later, rangers at two different parks told me that bikes were actually beneficial to trail maintenance. How? They flattened down hoofprints and other irregularities, thus improving the road surfaces. Believe selectively.

How These Chapters Are Arranged

Chapters 2 through 8 cover trails within Cleveland National Forest's more than 50,000 acres. The first chapters (2 through 6) have been developed around main forest entry areas that lead to the Main Divide Trail (3S04), a route that runs the length of the Santa Ana Mountains through Orange County and connects directly or indirectly with every trail and fire road in the forest. Chapters 7 and 8 cover single-track and downhill rides throughout the National Forest.

MAP 1   CLEVELAND NATIONAL FOREST

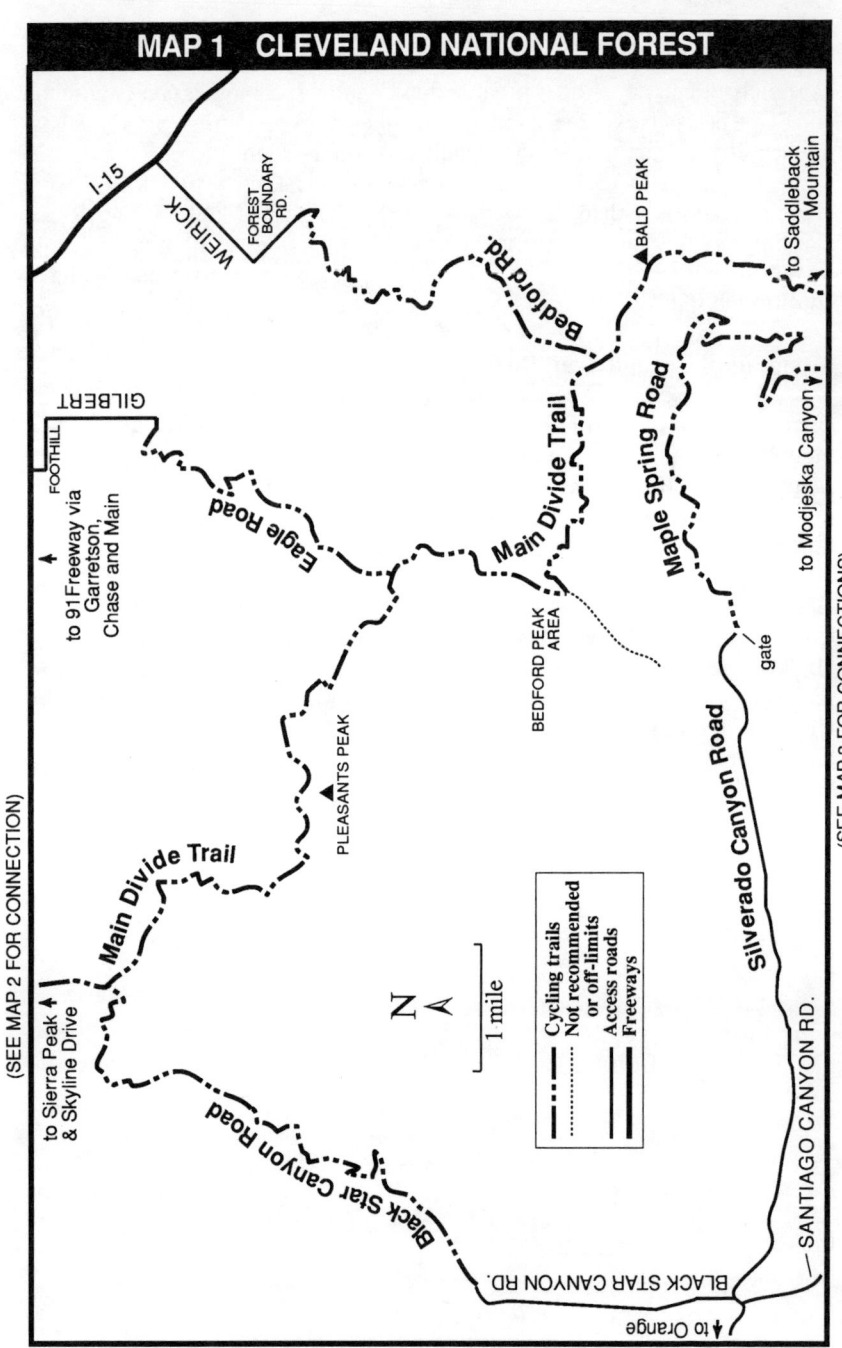

I-15

WEIRICK

FOREST
BOUNDARY
RD.

BALD PEAK

to Saddleback
Mountain

Bedford Rd.

GILBERT

FOOTHILL

to 91Freeway via
Garretson,
Chase and Main

Eagle Road

Main Divide Trail

Maple Spring Road

to Modjeska Canyon

BEDFORD PEAK
AREA

gate

(SEE MAP 3 FOR CONNECTIONS)

PLEASANTS PEAK

Main Divide Trail

(SEE MAP 2 FOR CONNECTION)

to Sierra Peak
& Skyline Drive

Silverado Canyon Road

N

1 mile

Cycling trails
Not recommended
or off-limits
Access roads
Freeways

Black Star Canyon Road

SANTIAGO CANYON RD.

BLACK STAR CANYON RD.

to Orange

18

CHAPTER 2

BLACK STAR CANYON

Early Canyon History

Early Spanish and Mexican settlers called this valley Cañada de los Indios (Indian Canyon). At the site of today's Hidden Ranch high in Black Star Canyon there was an Indian village located near a trail that lead from the sea across the mountains into Riverside County. Not all local Indians were pacified by Spanish/Mexican military power. Some escaped into California's mountains; others became fearsome bandits (like the famed half-breed Joaquin Murietta).

An early footnote of California history describes an 1831 expedition of American "Mountain Men" and local Mexican people who trailed a group of Indian horse thieves up Black Star Canyon. The group caught up with the Indians at Hidden Ranch, killed them, and recovered the lost animals.

Black Star Canyon received its present name in 1879 during the brief period when coal was mined at the Black Star Mine.

Note: A great deal of private property—ranches, residences, and recreational properties—is located within the National Forest. USFS Ranger Fran Caldwell suggests that visitors to the area obey all posted property signs and do not explore cabins or private structures, most of which are currently in use.

Getting There: Black Star Canyon is the northernmost entry point for reaching the Main Divide. From the city of Orange and the 55 Freeway take Chapman Avenue east. Chapman becomes Santiago Canyon Road after 4 or 5 miles. Continue approximately 5 more miles to the Silverado Canyon turnoff. As you turn onto Silverado note the sign for Black Star Canyon and make an immediate left, heading north on Black Star Canyon Road.

From I-5 in the Mission Viejo area take El Toro Road east approximately 7.6 miles to where it forks. Go left onto Santiago Canyon Road. Head north approximately 5 miles and turn onto Silverado Canyon Road. Then make a quick left and drive north to the metal pipe gate on Black Star Canyon Road.

Park off road. Take your bike past the gate (it's legal) and ride up the canyon. Because the surrounding area is private property, stay on the road. Also, watch for County fire closure signs in the dry season.

#1   Black Star Canyon to Main Divide Truck Trail

Mileage: 7 miles one way
Water: None
Level of Difficulty: Moderate, difficult
Elevation Gain: Begin: 1,000+ feet. Highest point: 3,045 feet. End: 1,000+ feet
Topo Maps: Orange County topo or USGS 7.5 min. (Black Star Canyon)
Campgrounds/Facilities: None
Nearest Services: Silverado Canyon

Take your bike through the steel pipe gate and proceed up the blacktop,

MAP 2 CLEVELAND NATIONAL FOREST

91 FREEWAY   Corona   to Riverside →

LINCOLN

SIERRA PEAK

Main Divide

Skyline Drive

to Black Star Canyon

CHASE DR.

N

1 mile

- - · · - - Cycling trails
─────── Access roads
━━━━━━━ Freeways

(SEE MAP 1 FOR CONNECTION)

bearing always to the right. The road continues gently uphill through the canyon, shaded by oak and sycamore trees (approximately 2 to 3 miles). Switchbacks rise steeply from the valley and the rider suddenly finds himself on chaparral-covered hillsides exposed to direct sun (unless you ride very early in the day). A long, tough climb continues past several ranches until you reach the Main Divide Truck Trail (3S04), at 2,815 foot elevation, 7 miles from the steel entry gate at Black Star Canyon. At the Main Divide Road find a good spot to rest from your climb. You may wish to begin your return from here back into Black Star Canyon.

Sierra Peak Option: To visit Sierra Peak, 3 miles north of the Black Star/ Main Divide crossroad, turn left at the junction with 3S04. Less than a mile north of the intersection you pass Skyline Drive (see next ride description). After the intersection, continue on to Sierra Peak. You can't miss it—it's a forest of communications antennae. The peak stands directly above the 91 Freeway, one of Orange County's busiest thoroughfares. You can see east and north Orange County, across to the Chino Hills and beyond to the San Gabriel Mountains. The towns of Riverside County appear just to the east.

Sierra Peak is a dead end for the mountain biker. The Main Divide Road then drops down into private land, where there's no entry. It's time to go home, but not before you enjoying the panoramic view.

#2   Black Star Canyon to Skyline Drive (1712) and Riverside County
Mileage: 13.5 miles
Water: None
Level of Difficulty: Difficult, moderate

Elevation: Begin: 1,000+ feet. Highest point: 2,815 feet. End: 1,100+ feet.
Topo Maps: Orange County topo or USGS 7.5 minute series (Black Star Canyon, Corona South)
Campgrounds/Facilities: None
Nearest Services: Silverado Canyon, Corona

Parking Your Second Car: Take the 91 Freeway east through Orange County into Corona. Exit right on Lincoln and travel approximately 2.5 miles south to Chase Drive. Turn right on Chase and then left onto Skyline Drive. Park off road near the trailhead.

Follow directions in Ride #1 to reach the Main Divide Truck Trail. Turn left and continue about 1 mile north along the Main Divide Trail to Skyline Drive. Turn right and head downhill. Skyline Drive drops less steeply than the other mountain roads leading out of the National Forest. Notice the farms and lushly irrigated areas around Corona as you lose altitude into the canyons below the Main Divide Truck Trail. On leaving Skyline Drive take note of the verdant orange groves tucked into ravines and steep-walled canyons along the way.

#3   Black Star Canyon to Eagle Road (4S07) and Riverside County
Mileage: 19.9 miles
Water: None
Level of Difficulty: Difficult
Elevation: Begin: 1,000+ feet. Highest point: 4,000+ feet. End: 1,400+ feet.
Topo Maps: Orange County topo or USGS 7.5 minute series (Black Star Canyon, Corona South)
Campgrounds/Facilities: None
Nearest Services: Silverado Canyon or Corona

Parking Your Second Car: Take the 55 Freeway to the 91 Freeway east toward Corona. Exit Main Street heading south for 2.5 miles. Make a left turn at Chase Drive. One-half mile later, turn right on Garretson, go 1.25 miles south. At Foothill Drive turn left and travel 0.5 mile to Gilbert Avenue. At Gilbert, turn right and drive 1 mile to the trailhead. Approximately 100 yards from the trailhead note an old wooden barn on the right. Park here. Do not park *between* the barn and the trailhead (almost 100 yards); the land is private.

Follow Ride #1 up Black Star Canyon to Main Divide Truck Trail. Turn right and continue 3.5 miles to Pleasants Peak where there is a divide in the road. Take the left fork that keeps you on the Main Divide Trail (the right fork dead-ends atop Pleasants Peak) and continue along the Main Divide Trail 3.9 more miles to Eagle Road (4S07). Turn left and begin a descent above Eagle Canyon. In 5.5 miles of ridge-top travel you come to the road's end in Riverside County. Follow the trail to your car.

This is a very physical ride. No sooner do you leave Black Star Canyon than you look south along the Main Divide. Many miles and over 1,400 feet of elevation await before Eagle Canyon. But, for those who attempt this challenge, the route is a visual delight. You can normally see San Gorgonio and San Jacinto Mountains from here, and the many canyons of the Santa Ana range make interesting viewing.

#4 Black Star Canyon to Bedford Canyon Road and Riverside County

Mileage: 23.4 miles
Water: None
Level of Difficulty: Difficult
Elevation: Begin: 1,000+ feet. High point: 4,000+ feet. End: 1,400+ feet.
Topo Maps: Orange County topo or USGS 7.5 minute series (Black Star Canyon, Corona South)
Campgrounds: None
Nearest Services: Silverado Canyon or Corona

Parking Your Second Car: Take the 55 Freeway to 91 East. Near Corona, head south on I-15. Exit from the I-15 Freeway onto Weirick. As the off ramp descends to street level, turn right on Weirick and make an immediate left turn onto Forest Boundary Road. Drive 0.5 miles to Bedford Road (small white metal sign next to large brickyard). Turn right. At first blacktop, the road soon becomes gravel and red clay, then red clay only. Though a short distance from the freeway, Bedford Road twists and winds its way into the hills, seemingly forever. The road is often in bad condition. Do not take your two-wheel drive vehicle there after a rain; you would certainly become bogged down in gooey red clay. Many private roads lead into Bedford Road. *Stay on the main track.* The Forest Service gate is 1.9 miles from the highway. Park approximately 0.5 mile below the gate on a saddle above an orchard. The road is narrow and without good parking.

Like the many rides along the Main Divide Truck Trail this route is physically demanding. As part of your reward, however, you travel a route that makes you feel as if you're pedaling "at the top of the world." The San Jacinto range to the east looks as though you might reach out and touch it. With your eyes you can follow the Temescal Valley (in Riverside County below) south where it becomes part of San Diego County. Finally, take a good look at the development of Bedford Canyon as you descend Bedford Road (to the left). Starting as a few modest watersheds, the canyon grows and widens. Finally steep slopes and sheer walls spew out the rocky debris, which becomes a massive flood plain emptying into Temescal Valley.

Follow the directions in Ride #1 and ride up through Black Star Canyon to the Main Divide Road. Turn right, riding in a twisting southerly direction for 10.9 miles—past Pleasants Peak, Eagle Road (4S07), Bedford Peak, and finally Bedford Road (4S03). Turn left on Bedford Road and glide 5.5 miles through Riverside County to the end of the trail. Perhaps *glide* is the wrong word for the twisting, rock-cluttered road plunging from the high ridge of the Santa Anas. The drop is fast and full of dangerous turns in places. At the end of 5.5 miles you come to the Forest Service gate across the road. Pass through the gate and continue riding down Bedford Road. One-half mile later you find your car.

#5 Black Star Canyon to Silverado Canyon or Modjeska Canyon

Mileage: 27.7 miles or 30.3 miles
Water: None/Silverado Canyon
Level of Difficulty: Experts only
Elevation: Begin: 1,000+ feet. Highest point: 4,523 feet. End: 1,500+ feet.
Topo Maps: Orange County topo or USGS 7.5 minute series (Black Star Canyon, Corona South, Santiago Peak)
Campgrounds: None
Nearest Services: Silverado Canyon

Parking Your Second Car (Silverado Canyon): See Ride #1, Chapter 3.

Parking Your Second Car (Modjeska Canyon): See Ride #1, Chapter 4.

Follow the driving and riding directions for Ride #1 to reach the intersection with Main Divide Truck Trail (7 miles at 2,815 feet). Turn right and begin a long climb of approximately 1,200 feet and 3.1 miles to Pleasants Peak (between Pleasants Peak and Bedford Peak you'll pass Eagle Road on your left, #4S07). The elevations drop nearly 400 feet to Bedford Peak, 4.5 miles distant. Along the way you have numerous minor elevation gains and losses. From Bedford Peak, the next measuring point is Bald Peak, 3.6 miles away. Between peaks you'll pass Bedford Road (4S03) on your left. Elevations are 3,639 feet on Bedford Road and max out at 3,947 feet on Bald Peak. Once again, uphill work is relentless on this high ridge of the Santa Anas. From Bald Peak climb south 2.5 miles to the junction of Main Divide Truck Trail north and south, Maple Spring Trail, and Harding Truck Trail. For Silverado Canyon turn right at the junction onto Maple Spring Road and head toward the pine trees below (7 miles). For Modjeska Canyon, turn right, drop down a slight incline and make a quick left turn. You'll face a gated road (Harding Truck Trail, 5S08), which drops quickly along a rocky ridge (9.3 miles to road's end).

Photo: Corey McTigue

CHAPTER 3

SILVERADO CANYON

This valley was known by the early Hispanic settlers as Cañada de la Madera (Timber Canyon). The trees in the valley and on the mountain above were cut to form the structural elements of Mission San Juan Capistrano and other early California buildings.

The canyon was renamed Silverado in 1877 after silver was discovered and mined there. More trees were felled to build mine shafts and a thriving city of 1,500 people. The valley boomed. Regular stage transport ran between Los Angeles and Santa Ana. After a few years the silver ore played out and the glory days of Silverado came to a close.

Climbing steadily through Silverado Canyon you pass shady glens, pleasant creeks and pine forests—the latter not immediately associated with this arid coastal region. Finally, you find panoramic beauty atop the highest ridges of the Santa Ana Mountains.

#1 Silverado Canyon to Maple Spring Trail and Return
Mileage: 16 miles maximum round trip (or turn back at any point)
Water: U.S. Forest Service Station, beginning of Silverado Canyon
Level of Difficulty: Beginner
Elevation: Begin 900+ feet. High point: 2,500+ feet. End: 900+ feet.
Topo Maps: Orange County topo or USGS 7.5 minute series (Santiago Peak, Corona South)
Campground/Facilities: None

Getting There: From the City of Orange and the 55 Freeway, take Chapman Avenue east. Chapman becomes Santiago Canyon Road after 5 miles. Continue another 5 miles to Silverado Canyon Road and turn left.

From the I-5 Freeway in the Mission Viejo area take El Toro Road east 7.6 miles to the fork. Go left onto Santiago Canyon Road. Drive north five miles to the Silverado Canyon exit and turn right.

Park at any one of numerous spots near the highway and bordering the Water District facilities.

The first 5.5 miles of the road into Silverado Canyon are on a two-lane blacktop highway. The first 2 or 3 miles are not particularly noteworthy. As you get in farther, however, you'll notice a mixture of old-fashioned and newer homes nestled between the canyon hillsides and Santiago Creek. Many of the old homes look like miniature dollhouses—so tiny, I've often wondered how the occupants were able to stand erect within. Silverado and surrounding canyons are home to the "horsey" set who prize their livestock, dogs, and secluded ranch lifestyle. Do not trespass on private land.

Moving farther down the canyon, the pavement ends at a metal pipe Forest Service gate. Maple Spring Road (5S04) begins here as a dirt road.

Beyond this spot there are no homes, the canyon narrows and the oak trees grow tall and thick along Silverado Creek. The road curves its way gently through the valley, and the sounds of birds and creek predominate. The ride continues in this way for another 2 to 3 miles past the gate. Finally, you cross the creek, make a sharp right turn and begin a steep climb up the hill. I recommend that beginners turn around at this point and return to their car. Grab a cold drink in one of the stores in the canyon or something to eat at the local cafe.

#2 Silverado Canyon to Modjeska Canyon

Mileage: 16 miles
Water: At Silverado and Modjeska Canyon
Level of Difficulty: Moderate, difficult
Elevation: Begin: 1,800+ feet. High point: 4,523 feet. End: 1,500+ feet.
Topo Maps: Orange County topo or USGS 7.5 minute series (Santiago Peak, Corona South)
Campground and Facilities: None
Nearest Services: Silverado Canyon

Parking Your Second Car: From the 55 Freeway take Chapman Avenue east. After 4 to 5 miles Chapman becomes Santiago Canyon Road. Continue another 8 miles east or so to Modjeska Canyon Road. Turn left, driving 2 more miles to the Tucker Wildlife Sanctuary and park.

From I-5 in the Mission Viejo area, turn off on El Toro Road and head east 7.6 miles to the fork. Go left onto Santiago Canyon Road and head north approximately 2 miles. Turn right onto Modjeska Canyon Road, heading 2 miles more inland to the Tucker Wildlife Sanctuary (parking).

Drive your other vehicle to Silverado Canyon and up to the pipe gate (see Ride #1). Ride up Maple Spring Trail in the cool shade of the tree-lined canyon. Within a few miles the road climbs steeply up a ridge out of the shaded protection of the valley. From this point you begin a long, steady climb into chaparral country. The mountain road has a southern exposure and can be uncomfortably warm. The track, however, is well graded and well suited to continuous ascent.

Another couple of miles and you see the first isolated stands of Coulter pines and spruce on the high mountainsides. Remembering that these valleys and mountains were covered with timber gives you some insight into the massive ecological changes caused here by Western "civilization."

Approximately 7 miles from the steel pipe gate in Silverado you reach a high saddle (4,500 feet) that is a junction of four trails. Note a road to your right closed off by a steel pipe gate. This is 5S08, the Harding Truck Trail, which leads down to Modjeska Canyon (approximately 9.3 miles). The trip up takes several hours, and the downside seems like about 5 minutes as you brake, turn, and dodge for dear life. Though a relatively well graded road, there is a lot of rocky rubble necessitating extreme caution on your part. (I planted my helmet into a pile of stones there once and still managed to come out smilin'.) You can see a long way downhill, which makes the run safer vis-a-vis uphill climbing riders. Since Harding Truck Trail is gated, there is no vehicular traffic. Soon your downhill glide is ended and you pick up your second vehicle.

#3   Silverado Canyon to Black Star Canyon
Mileage: 27 miles
Water: None (Silverado Canyon)
Level of Difficulty: Difficult, moderate (using car shuttle)
Topo Maps: Orange County topo or USGS 7.5 minute series (Santiago Peak, Corona South, Black Star Canyon)
Elevation: Begin 1,800+ feet. Highest point: 4,523 feet. End: 1,000+ feet.

This route is the reverse of the Black Star Canyon to Silverado, described in Chapter 2. However, there are two major differences. First, this ride has more downhill (my favorite!); secondly, you can shave 7 miles off the route by driving up the Maple Spring Trail to the Main Divide Trail, where you can park your car and begin riding. Make a left turn onto Main Divide Trail (3S04) heading ultimately toward Black Star Canyon. There are still several elevation gains along the route. Between Bald and Pleasant peaks there are numerous 50-foot to 300-foot gains and losses. This makes for an interesting though much less physically demanding outing. The views from this high ridge are stunning, and the car shuttle up Maple Spring Trail changes the trip from a "grunt" to a "jaunt" (depending on your level of commitment to physical suffering).

One mile west of Bald Peak you cross Bedford Road (4S03). The next major mountain you pass is Bedford Peak. Continue bearing right on 3S04. A

Photo: Robert Rasmussen

short distance from Bedford Peak, Eagle Road (4S07) leads down into Riverside County. Pass it and continue on 3S04 toward Pleasants Peak, the next major mountain at 4,007 foot elevation. This is the highest point along the high ridge of the Santa Ana Mountains north of the trail junction of Main Divide Truck Trail north and south, Harding Truck Trail and Maple Spring Trail. From here it's downhill to Black Star Canyon Road (82) Turn left at Black Star Canyon Road and begin a 7 mile drop to your car and home.

#4   Silverado Canyon to Bedford Canyon

Mileage: Route A: 16.5 miles (bike all the way). Route B: 9.5 miles (car shuttle to Main Divide/Four-Way Trail Junction)
Water: None
Level of Difficulty: Route A is difficult; Route B is moderate
Elevation: Begin 1,800+ feet. High point: 4,523 feet. End: 1,400+ feet.
Topo Maps: Orange County topo or USGS 7.5 minute series (Santiago Peak, Corona South)
Campgrounds: None
Nearest Services: Beginning of Silverado Canyon and in Corona

Parking Your Second Car: Take the 55 Freeway to 91 Freeway east. Turn south on I-15 and drive south 5 miles, exiting on Weirick. Turn immediately left on Forest Boundary Road. One-half mile from the Weirick off ramp is Bedford Road (small white metal sign next to a large brick yard). Turn right and follow this road 1.9 miles to a saddle area 0.5 miles below the trailhead. Park here. There is no parking near the Forest Service gate.

Drive up Silverado Canyon (see Ride #1) to the pipe gate and take Maple Spring Trail to the four-way trail junction with Main Divide Truck Trail north/south and Harding Truck Trail. Turn left (north) on the Main Divide Truck Trail (3S04) and travel 2.5 miles to Bald Peak. Here the road veers sharply left toward the northwest. One mile beyond, you'll see Bedford Canyon Road (4S03). Turn right and begin the 2,000 foot drop into Riverside County. Pick up your car below the trailhead gate. (Special note: Frequent Flier credit is available from most airlines for this "E ticket" experience.)

#5   Silverado Canyon to Indian Truck Trail

Mileage: Route A is 20.5 miles; Route B is 9.5 miles
Water: None
Level of Difficulty: Route A is difficult; Route B is intermediate, due to car shuttle from four-way road junction
Elevation: Begin 1,800+ feet. High point: 5,400+ feet. End: 1,200+ feet.
Topo Maps: Orange County topo or USGS 7.5 minute series (Santiago Peak, Corona South, Alberhill)
Campground Facilities: None
Nearest Services: Temescal Valley area

Parking Your Second Car: Take the 55 Freeway to 91 Freeway east. Travel past Corona to the I-15 Freeway and turn south. Approximately 6 to 7 miles south of the 91 Freeway take the Indian Truck Trail turnoff. Turn right at the bottom of the off ramp. It immediately becomes a dirt road. Travel 0.5 miles to the fork in the road, take the left fork at the blue and white sign. Travel another 1.6 miles to the trailhead (just past the Korean religious center). Park 80 yards below the Forest Service gate.

Route A: Beginning at the metal pipe gate in Silverado Canyon (see Ride #1), travel 7 miles up Maple Spring Road (5S04) to junction with Main Divide Truck Trail (3S04). Going up a slight incline at the junction, turn right on the Main Divide Trail and travel 4 miles farther (plus 800+ elevation gain) to Saddleback Mountain/Santiago Peak.

The first 11 miles of this ride to Saddleback Mountain are tough. That distance also takes you nearly 3,700 feet up, enabling you to see a great many sights. The steep canyons within the Santa Ana Mountains seem to grow increasingly large as you pedal up Maple Spring Trail. Crossing over onto the Main Divide Road (3S04) between Modjeska and Santiago peaks, new sights appear. South and central Orange County lie below. The ocean appears beyond the coast and Catalina Island rises from the blue waters. Looking north you see the vastness of Los Angeles County.

Near the top of the mountain, the road forks right and left. Take the left— a steep downhill of over 1,900 feet in 4 miles. As your road (3S04) splits off from Saddleback Mountain, it's time to lower your seat and tighten your helmet. I dumped my bike twice going down this road and can attest to the fact that it is "user hostile." The road is steep and viciously rock-strewn. The only sights you'll be seeing for the next few miles will be around the front tire of your bike. The road is brutal and merits your utmost caution.

At the Indian Truck Trail (5S01) turn left and begin a long, 5.5 mile descent to the Temescal Canyon.

Route B: Drive one vehicle to Santiago Peak and park. Ride the short distance down to the fork in the road. Turn right and begin the murderous descent on 3S04 to Indian Truck Trail. Take a left at the junction (5S01) and drop 5.5 miles to the Forest Service gate.

#6 Silverado Canyon to Eagle Canyon
Mileage: Route A is 20.5 miles (bike all the way); Route B is 13.5 miles (car shuttle to Main Divide Junction)
Water: Silverado Canyon
Level of Difficulty: Route A is difficult; Route B is moderate
Elevation: Begin: 1,800+ feet. High point: 4,523 feet. End: 1,400+ feet.
Topo Maps: Orange County topo or USGS 7.5 minute series (Santiago Peak, Corona South)
Campgrounds: None
Nearest Services: Silverado Canyon, Corona

Photo: Robert Rasmussen

Parking Your Second Car: Take the 55 Freeway to the 91 Freeway east toward Corona. Exit Main Street and head south 2.5 miles. Make a left turn at Chase Drive. One-half mile later turn right on Garretson, go 1.25 miles south. At Foothill Drive turn left and travel 0.5 miles to Gilbert Avenue. At Gilbert, turn right and continue 1 mile to the trailhead. One hundred yards from the trailhead note an old wooden barn on the right. Park here. The land between it and the trailhead (approximately 100 yards) is private. You may not park there. You may, however, cross the private land to enter the National Forest as long as you remain *on the road.*

Drive up Silverado Canyon (see Ride #1) and take the Maple Spring Trail (past the metal gate) 7 miles to the four-way trail junction. Turn left on the Main Divide Truck Trail (3S04). Travel northwest along the high ridge 3.5 miles. You will pass Bedford Road (4S03). Keep going another 3.9 miles to Eagle Road (4S07). Turn right and begin your long descent (4.4 miles and over 2,000 feet down). The 7-mile ride to the Main Divide Trail is a long and challenging one. The elevation gain is impressive, as are the views.

However, there are more important considerations in mountain biking— like riding downhill. After you reach the Main Divide Trail, the road drops over 500 feet in elevation within 2.5 miles, making for "Fright Night" acceleration while you simultaneously try to evade rocks and sand traps. There are a couple of spots north of Bald Mountain requiring short uphill climbs. The rest of the road descends modestly until Eagle Road. There the path drops like a stone until reaching "Greater Metropolitan Corona" below.

#7 Silverado Canyon to Santiago Peak and Return

Mileage: 22 miles round trip
Water: Silverado Canyon
Level of Difficulty: Moderate, difficult
Elevation: Begin: 1,800+ feet. High point: 5,687 feet. End: 1,800+ feet.
Topo Maps: Orange County topo or USGS 7.5 minute series (Santiago Peak, Corona South)
Campgrounds/Facilities: None
Nearest Services: Silverado Canyon

Getting There: See Ride #1, this chapter. Drive up Silverado Canyon to the metal pipe gate.

Begin your trip to Saddleback by heading up Maple Spring Trail to the Main Divide Truck Trail (3S04) and a four-way trail junction. Ascend a slight incline, and make a quick right onto the Main Divide Truck Trail (#3S04). Ride south toward Santiago Peak, the highest part of Saddleback Mountain. Four miles and about 1,000 feet more of elevation gain puts you atop Santiago Peak, up a short spur road form the Main Divide Trail.

Depending upon air quality, the views are spectacular. Walk around the peak. Note Catalina Island across the way. Orange County, Los Angeles and Riverside counties lie before you. Drink to replace lost fluids and eat to regain used nutrients. Take a couple "cheesecake" photos for posterity and even some landscape shots—you know, the kind that seem so good in the viewfinder but come back looking like satellite photos of earth.

Return to Silverado Canyon by the same route. Coming down off the peak, be sure to take the left fork of 3S04. (A right turn will drop you off on the wrong side of the mountain and you will have to retrace your steps uphill.) Continue to the four-way trail junction and turn left onto Maple Spring Trail. Go straight downhill toward the stands of pine trees. Avoid road hazards on the descent. Seven miles and seemingly a few moments later you will reach your car.

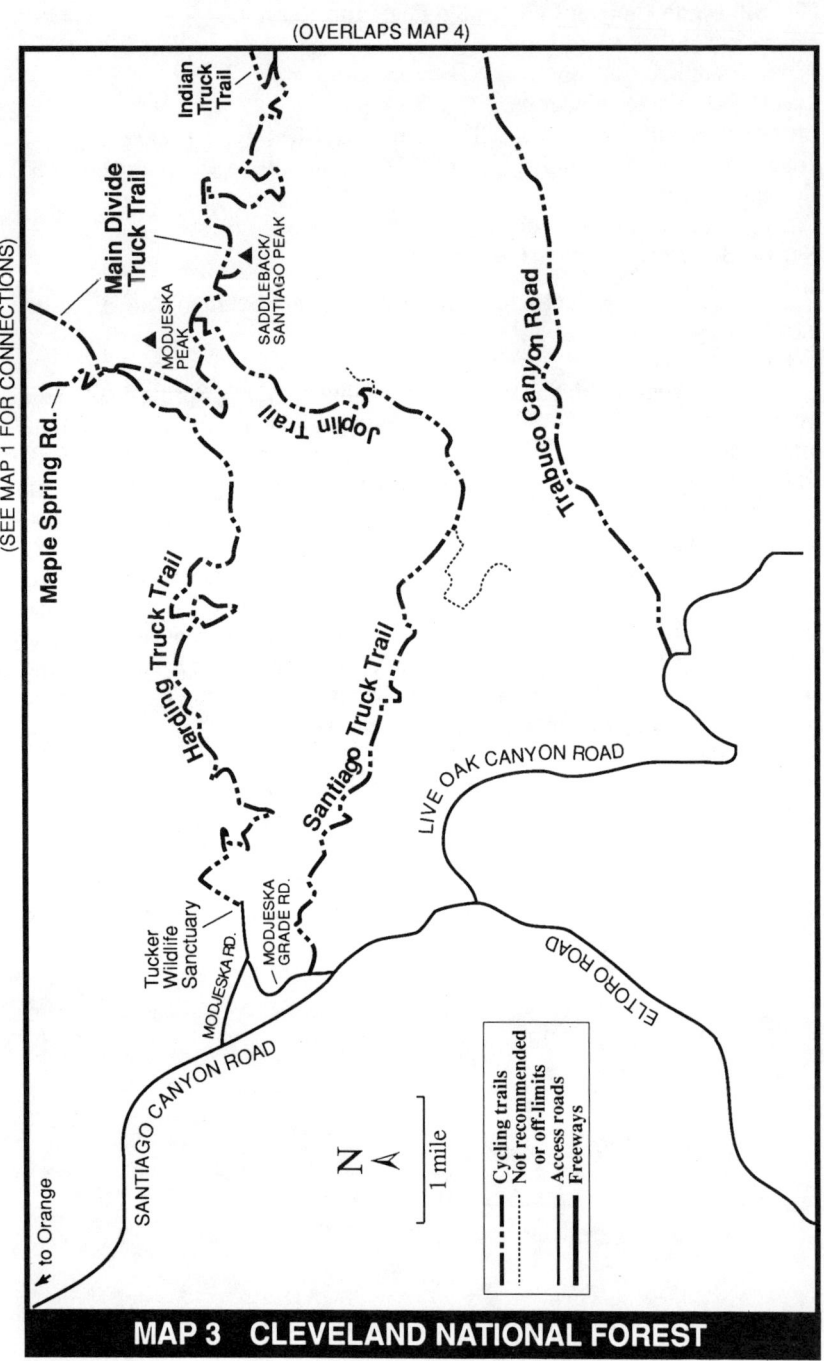

Indian Truck Trail

Main Divide Truck Trail

SADDLEBACK/ SANTIAGO PEAK

MODJESKA PEAK

Joplin Trail

Trabuco Canyon Road

Maple Spring Rd.

(SEE MAP 1 FOR CONNECTIONS)

Harding Truck Trail

Santiago Truck Trail

LIVE OAK CANYON ROAD

Tucker Wildlife Sanctuary

MODJESKA RD.

MODJESKA GRADE RD.

EL TORO ROAD

SANTIAGO CANYON ROAD

to Orange

N

1 mile

Cycling trails
Not recommended or off-limits
Access roads
Freeways

MAP 3   CLEVELAND NATIONAL FOREST

CHAPTER 4

MODJESKA CANYON

Modjeska Canyon is another of Orange County's cozy riparian valleys. It is named for Helena Modjeska, a Polish immigrant actress who found success on the American stage. Madame Modjeska purchased several hundred acres of land in the canyon and built an estate named "Arden," in reference to the forest of Arden in Shakespeare's comedy, *As You Like It*. The home is currently undergoing restoration as a historic monument.

The life of the free-spirited actress is today honored by a group called the Daughters of Helena Modjeska, Orange County women who host stultifying luncheons at which they wear funny hats and consume vast amounts of tea.

#1   Modjeska Canyon to Santiago Peak via Harding Truck Trail

Mileage: 26.6 miles round trip
Water: Modjeska Canyon at the Wildlife Sanctuary
Level of Difficulty: Moderate, difficult
Elevation: Begin: 1,500+ feet. High point: 5,687 feet. End: 1,500+ feet.
Topo Maps: Orange County topo or USGS 7.5 minute series (Santiago Peak)
Campground/Facilities: None
Nearest Services: Silverado Canyon, Cook's Corner (Mission Viejo)

Getting There: From the 55 Freeway, take Chapman Avenue east. After 5 miles Chapman becomes Santiago Canyon Road. Continue another 8.7 miles east to Modjeska Canyon Road. Turn left, drive 2 more miles to the Tucker Wildlife Sanctuary.

From Mission Viejo and the I-5 Freeway, exit on El Toro Road, heading inland. 7.6 miles east of I-5, El Toro Road splits in two. Take the left fork, Santiago Canyon Road. Drive north 2 miles. Turn right on Modjeska Canyon Road and head 2 miles farther to the Tucker Wildlife Sanctuary.

Park your car properly. Just beyond the lot you'll see a metal pipe gate and the beginning of Harding Truck Trail (5S08), which heads up to the Main Divide Truck Trail.

Take your bicycle past the gate and begin a relentless climb. Harding Truck Trail 5S08 from the Tucker Wildlife Sanctuary rises sharply from the parking lot at Modjeska Canyon's end. Within a few minutes you climb sharply up through the chaparral-covered mountainsides ever higher. The trail snakes along the hillside gaining elevation all along the way. Looking below and several hundred feet to your right, you'll see the Santiago Truck Trail.

After 9.3 grueling miles you'll come to the four-way trail junction. Pass through the metal gate that separates the Harding Trail from the other roads. Turn right, climbing up a small incline to the junction. Turn right again. You are now riding south on the Main Divide Truck Trail (3S04).

Continue 4 miles along the road making slight elevation gains. Suddenly

Santiago Peak (the highest portion of Saddleback Mountain) looms ahead and you face a strong climb to the top of the peak.

Two hundred yards or so from the top of the mountain the trail splits in two. The left fork is the continuation of the Main Divide Truck Trail (heading south). This trail drops profoundly down one side of the mountain becoming one of the roughest routes I've ever encountered. Take the right fork. You will quickly reach the top of Santiago Peak.

When the air is clear, the views from this peak are outstanding. Looking across the water you can see Catalina Island, to the east are Mt. San Gorgonio and Mt. San Jacinto (over 60 miles distant), to the south you can look many miles into San Diego County. To the north are the suburban sprawl and high rise buildings of Los Angeles County. Long Beach Harbor and the Palos Verdes Peninsula are clearly visible.

As you leave the peak be sure to bear left (west) on the Main Divide Road to return to your car. Ride 4 miles to the four-way trail junction. Turn left. Descend the small incline, make another quick left. You'll see the metal gate and sign for 5S08. Begin the long drop toward Modjeska Canyon.

#2 Modjeska Canyon to Silverado Canyon

Mileage: 16.3 miles (to Silverado gate)
Water: Modjeska Canyon; Silverado Canyon (near highway)
Level of Difficulty: Moderate, difficult
Elevation: Begin: 1,500+ feet. High point: 4,523 feet. End: approximately 1,500+ feet.
Topo Maps: Orange County topo or USGS 7.5 minute series (Santiago Peak, Corona South)
Campgrounds/Facilities: None
Nearest Services: Silverado Canyon

Parking Your Second Car. From the City of Orange and the 55 Freeway, take Chapman Avenue east. Chapman becomes Santiago Canyon Road after 5 miles. Continue another 5 miles to Silverado Canyon Road and turn left.

From I-5 in the Mission Viejo area take El Toro Road east for 7.6 miles until it forks. Take the left fork, which is Santiago Canyon Road. Drive north five miles to the Silverado Canyon exit and turn right.

Park at any one of numerous spots near the highway and bordering the Water District facilities.

Drive to Modjeska Canyon as described in Ride #1 and ride up Harding Truck Trail. The cool riparian valley soon changes to steep, brush-covered hillsides. As you gain elevation, your perception of the area grows accordingly: narrow valleys are transformed into broad gorges; hillsides become steep mountainsides dropping thousands of feet to the canyons below.

Ride 9.3 miles to the Harding Truck Trail gate (5S08). There is a junction of trails on a small saddle there. A look to the east shows the high ridges and steep valleys of the Santa Anas, as well as the San Gabriel and San Bernardino mountains.

Seven miles from the trailhead you'll arrive at the gated entrance to Maple Spring Road/Silverado Canyon. On the way you pass through stands of pine trees and the forested groves along Santiago Creek. A short distance west of the metal gate are two "God-sent" opportunities to grab a "cold one." Two convenience stores are located on the Silverado Canyon Road as well as a small restaurant. You'll be wanting something to drink by the end of your ride!

#3 Modjeska Canyon to Black Star Canyon
Mileage: 31 miles
Water: Modjeska Canyon only. Carry 3 to 4 quarts.
Level of Difficulty: Difficult
Elevation: Begin: 1,500+ feet. High point: 4,523 feet. End: 1,800+ feet.
Topo Maps: Orange County topo or USGS 7.5 minute series (Santiago Peak, Corona South, Black Star Canyon)
Campgrounds/Facilities: None
Nearest Services: Silverado Canyon

Parking Your Second Car: From the city of Orange and the 55 Freeway take Chapman Avenue east. Chapman becomes Santiago Canyon after 4 to 5 miles. Continue approximately 5 more miles to the Silverado Canyon and turn left. Then take an immediate left again onto Black Star Canyon Road and head north to the metal pipe gate.

From the I-5 Freeway in the Mission Viejo area, take the El Toro Road exit and head inland approximately 7.6 miles east to where El Toro Road forks. Go left onto Santiago Canyon Road. Head north approximately 5 miles to the Silverado Canyon exit. Make a right then a quick left and drive north to the metal pipe gate on Black Star Canyon Road.

Park off road. Take your bike past the gate (it's legal) and head up the canyon. Because the surrounding area is private property, stay on the road. Also, watch for County fire closure signs in dry season.

Drive up Modjeska Canyon and ascend the Harding Truck Trail (5S08) 9.3 miles to the saddle and four-way trail junction as described in Ride #1. As you climb the road, the narrow canyon changes to a spectacular view of rugged valleys and steep mountainsides surrounding you. At the saddle pause for a moment to look west. Central Orange County covers the lowlands before you. The ocean lies just beyond.

Turn right, climbing briefly to Main Divide Truck Trail #3S04. Then turn left and begin a "long screaming power dive" 2.5 miles and approximately 600 feet to Bald Peak, a fabulous downhill run though extreme caution is advised due to road conditions. From here the road meanders atop the high ridges. It is from Bald Peak to Bedford Peak that the downhill fun continues against a backdrop of Southern California's lofty mountain ranges in the distance.

North of Bedford Peak the downhill party's over and it's time to put those "climin' shoes" back on. The trail intermittently ascends and descends seesawing until you reach Pleasants Peak. Several hundred-foot drops and gains are what you can look forward to between Bedford and Pleasant peaks.

The Pleasants Peak area is a good spot to rest and survey your accomplishments. A look west shows the rugged interior canyons of the Santa Anas. A view east finds more spectacular Santa Ana Mountain's scenery. The lowland communities of Riverside County stretch away from the foot of the mountains and a glance south peers into San Diego County.

After Pleasants Peak it's "Freebie" time for the weary rider. A downhill run begins at Pleasants Peak and doesn't end until the gate at Black Star Canyon.

From Modjeska Canyon to the four-way trail junction is 9.3 miles. The great drop to Bald Peak totals 11.8 miles. Continuing west find Bedford Road at 12.8 miles (4S03). Ride farther west. At 16.7 miles pass Eagle Canyon Road (4S07). Continue along the Main Divide to Pleasants Peak (it has radio towers and a road junction). The junction makes 20.6 miles. Take the right fork. At 23.7 miles Black Star Canyon Road (82) appears on your left as well as Beek's Place, a group of ruins dating back to the turn of the century. The end is near, for it's downhill all the way into Black Star Canyon.

#4   Modjeska Canyon to Bedford Road
Mileage: 18 miles
Water: None (Modjeska only)
Level of Difficulty: Difficult, moderate
Elevation: Begin: 1,800+ feet. High point: 4,523 feet. End: 1,400+ feet.
Topo Maps: Orange County topo or USGS 7.5 minute series (Santiago Peak, Corona South)
Campgrounds: None
Nearest Services: Silverado Canyon and Corona

Parking Your Second Car: Take the 55 Freeway to 91 Freeway east. Turn south on I-15 and drive about 5 miles, exiting on Weirick. Turn immediately left onto Forest Boundary Road. One-half mile later turn right on Bedford Road (small white metal road sign next to a large brickyard). Follow this road 1.9 miles to a saddle area 0.5 miles below the Forest Service gate.

From the parking area of the Tucker Wildlife Sanctuary in Modjeska Canyon, go through the metal pipe gate and begin riding the Harding Truck Trail (5S08) 9.3 miles to the four-way trail junction. Turn right up a slight incline to another dirt road. This road is the Main Divide Truck Trail (3S04). Turn left (north), beginning a long, 2.5 mile downhill run to Bald Peak. All along the Main Divide Trail the roads are rocky, demanding caution on the rider's part. In dry weather, patches of soil along this route turn sandy and become dangerous. Riders with narrow tires could lose control in these seasonal sand traps. As you hit one of these things at high speed and can feel yourself beginning to lose it, you'll know exactly what I mean. This is no time to test your helmet on the rocks. So ride safely. There is an unmistakable feeling of "flying" as you descend 500+ feet to Bald Mountain. Your speed plus the ridge-top illusion of being at the top of the world make for an exciting experience. There is a sensation of freedom riding on the Main Divide Trail. In fact, another "freefall" descent awaits you beyond Bald Peak.

One mile east of Bald Peak lies Bedford Canyon Road (4S03). Turn right and begin the "Big Drop" (5.5 miles and approximately 2,300 feet), following the road to your car on the saddle above the orchard 0.5 miles from the Forest Service gate.

#5   Modjeska Canyon to Eagle Road (4S03)

Mileage: 22.5 miles
Water: Modjeska only
Level of Difficulty: Difficult
Elevation: Begin: 1,800+ feet. High point: 4,523 feet. End: 1,400+ feet.
Topo Maps: Orange County topo or USGS 7.5 minute series (Santiago Peak, Corona South)
Campgrounds: None
Nearest Services: Corona and Silverado Canyon

Parking Your Second Car: Take the 55 Freeway to the 91 Freeway east toward Corona. Exit Main Street heading south 2.5 miles. Go left at Chase Drive. One-half mile later turn right on Garretson, go 1.25 miles south. At Foothill Drive turn left. Go 0.5 miles to Gilbert. At Gilbert turn right. Follow the road one more mile to the trailhead. One hundred yards from the trailhead note an old wooden barn on the right. Park there in the barn area. The land between the barn and the trailhead (about 100 yards) is private. Do not park there.

This ride is a study in contrasts. The first part is a slow, exhausting climb of many miles and almost 3,000 feet in elevation gain. The rugged valleys and mountains of the western Santa Anas are the rider's primary vistas. The second part of the trip has a lot of fast downhill work. The views from Bald Peak and beyond are far-ranging. You can see three distant mountain ranges as well as the broad lowlands of Riverside County.

From the parking lot at Tucker Wildlife Refuge (see Ride #1) go through the metal gate onto the Harding Truck Trail (5S08). After 9 miles, reach the four-way trail junction. Turn right going up a short incline to another road (Main Divide Truck Trail #3S04). Turn left immediately and start the 2.5-mile downhill run to Bald Peak. From Bald Peak, the trail twists and turns atop the high ridge. At 11.8 miles you pass Bedford Road (4S03). Riding farther to 13.3 miles see Eagle Road (4S07) on your right. Turn right and begin descending a slowly dropping ridge line above Eagle Canyon (seen below and to your left). Remember, between Bald Peak and Bedford Peak there are numerous ascents of 50 to 300 feet.

#6   Modjeska Canyon to Indian Truck Trail (5S01)

Mileage: 24.8 miles
Water: None
Level of Difficulty: Difficult
Elevation: Begin: 1,500+ feet. High point: 5,400 feet. End: 1,200+ feet.
Topo Maps: Orange County topo or USGS 7.5 minute series (Santiago Peak, Alberhill)
Campgrounds/Facilities: None
Nearest Services: Temescal Valley area

Parking Your Second Car: Take the 55 Freeway to the 91 Freeway east. Travel past Corona and go south on the I-15 Freeway approximately 7 miles to the Indian Truck Trail turnoff. Turn right on the off ramp. The pavement turns to a dirt road. One-half mile from the pavement, the road forks at a blue and white sign. Take the left fork. 1.6 miles later find the trailhead just beyond the religious center.

Ride up the Harding Truck Trail (5S08) 9.3 miles to the four-way trail junction. The ride up Harding Trail is slow and laborious. Giant canyons rise around you as you progress steadily upward. A glimpse of suburban Orange County appears to the west over the ridges.

Go up a small incline and turn right on the Main Divide Truck Trail (3S04). Follow this road up and around Modjeska Peak to Santiago Peak 4 miles (800+ feet elevation gain). As you ride around Modjeska Peak, the vista unfolds more fully. You can see larger sections of south and central Orange County. The ocean stretches to the horizon.

Before reaching the top of Santiago Peak, the road forks. Take the left branch, but before you make the descent look south to the depths of Holy Jim and Trabuco canyons. To the left of the canyons watch the Main Divide Trail snake along the top of the high ridges of the eastern Santa Anas.

At this point, there can be no confusion as to where you're going (down). The road twists and turns over some of the roughest, rockiest, and brutal surface I have ever experienced. Experts should have no problem. Intermediate riders must exercise due caution. The challenge is undeniable as you drop like a stone 1,900+ feet and 4 miles down the Main Divide (that portion extending east of Santiago Peak).

After this 4-mile downhill run, turn left on Indian Truck Trail (5S01) and begin another plunge. The road twists and turns atop a descending ridge line for about 2,500 feet and 5.5 miles to Temescal Valley below. Follow the road to your second parked vehicle.

Probably no one in your party will volunteer to bicycle back to Modjeska Canyon at day's end.

#7 Santiago Truck Trail

Mileage: 13 miles round trip
Water: None
Level of Difficulty: Moderate
Elevation: Begin: 1,600+ feet. High point: 3,400+ feet. End: 1,600+ feet.
Topo Maps: Orange County topo or USGS 7.5 minute series (Santiago Peak)
Campgrounds/Facilities: None
Nearest Services: Mission Viejo

Getting There: From the 55 Freeway in Orange, take Chapman Avenue east. Chapman becomes Santiago Canyon Road after 5 miles. Continue 9.1 miles to Modjeska Grade Road, turn right, and find a metal gate on your right in about 1/4 mile.

From I-5 in Mission Viejo take El Toro Road 7.6 miles east to the fork. Go left onto Santiago Canyon Road, and in 0.9 miles turn right at Modjeska Grade Road. The gate is on the right about 1/4 mile up.

Park your car along the blacktop. Do not park in the trailhead driveway; your car will be ticketed or towed.

Enter the gate, take the dirt road to your right and ride up into the hills. The road snakes up the contours of the hill. Look above and to your left where you will catch glimpses of the Harding Truck Trail climbing above you towards Saddleback Mountain. The Santiago Truck Trail climbs the high ridge above Mission Viejo. The views below expand with your upward progress, with suburban and canyon views growing to become grand vistas.

At 6.5 miles you come to the Joplin Road, which drops sharply downhill and dead-ends. Don't make the mistake of taking it. There is no exit.

Santiago Truck Trail forks one mile beyond Joplin Road. Take the left fork that drops into a small valley ending at Old Camp, said to be the site of an ancient Indian hunting camp. (The right fork dead-ends into the mountain.) Joplin Foot Trail, which climbs sharply up from Old Camp to Saddleback Mountain, will be discussed in more detail in Chapter 7.

Retrace your steps back to your car after a thoroughly enjoyable ride.

Comments: In dry seasons Santiago Truck Trail may occasionally be closed by the Orange County Fire Marshal. (You can't miss the sign if it is.)

Joplin Road dead-ends into the Joplin Boys Ranch (i.e., prison). No wonder free access is frowned upon! While scouting the area I saw numerous parents leaving the ranch, teary-eyed, mascara streaked, solemn faced. Heartache hangs over the place like a dark cloud.

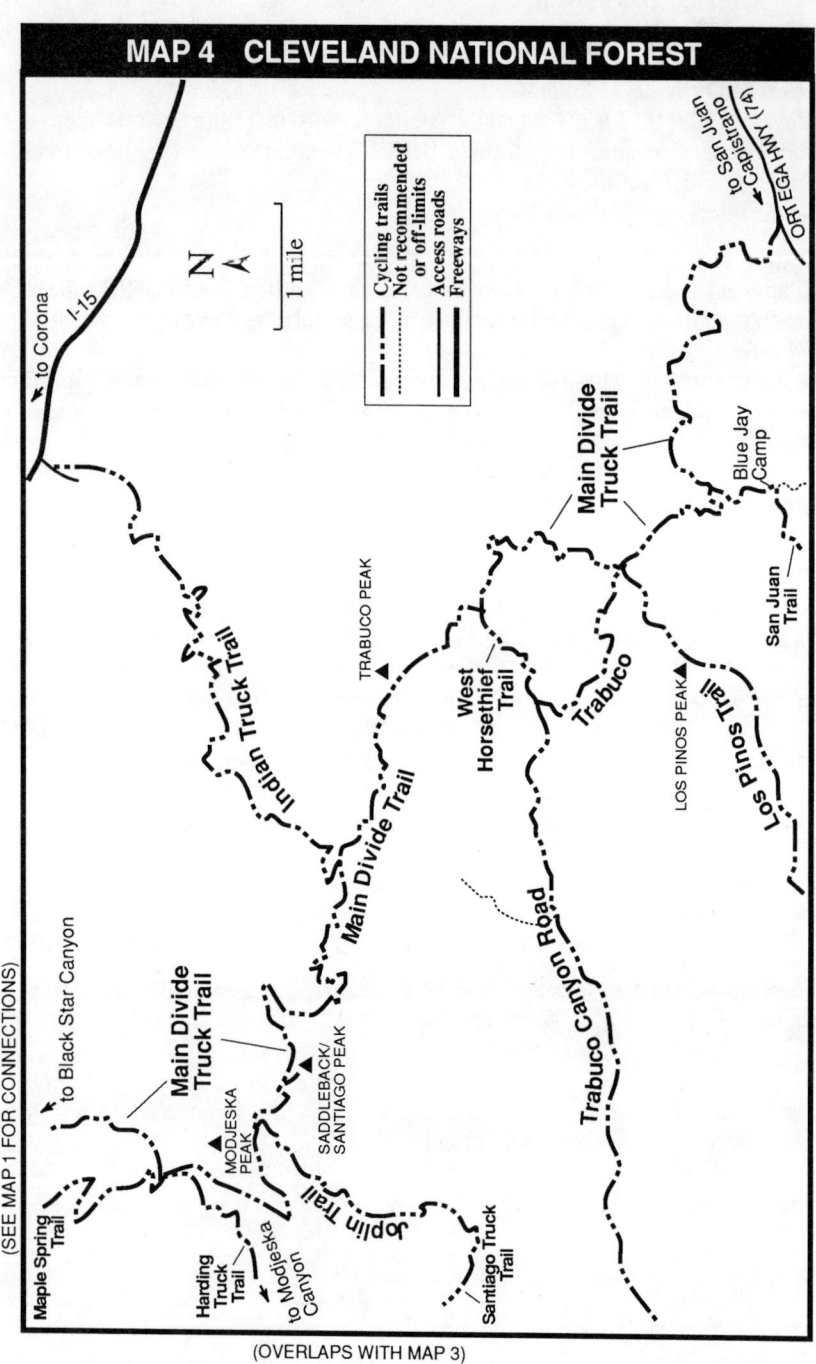

MAP 4 CLEVELAND NATIONAL FOREST

Cycling trails
Not recommended
or off-limits
Access roads
Freeways

N

1 mile

to Corona

I-15

to San Juan
Capistrano

ORTEGA HWY (74)

Main Divide
Truck Trail

Blue Jay
Camp

San Juan
Trail

TRABUCO PEAK

West
Horsethief
Trail

Trabuco

Indian Truck Trail

Main Divide Trail

LOS PINOS PEAK

Los Pinos Trail

Main Divide
Truck Trail

to Black Star Canyon

MODJESKA
PEAK

SADDLEBACK/
SANTIAGO PEAK

Maple Spring
Trail

Harding
Truck
Trail

to Modjeska
Canyon

Joplin Trail

Santiago Truck
Trail

Trabuco Canyon Road

(SEE MAP 1 FOR CONNECTIONS)

(SEE MAP 5 FOR CONNECTIONS)

(OVERLAPS WITH MAP 3)

CHAPTER 5

MAIN DIVIDE TRUCK TRAIL: SOUTH ENTRY

#1 South Main Divide Trail to Blue Jay Camp

Mileage: 6 miles one way (with car shuttle) or 12 miles round trip
Water: Blue Jay Camp / El Cariso Ranger Station
Level of Difficulty: Beginner
Elevation: Begin: 2,800+ feet. High point: 3,500+ feet. End: 2,800+ feet.
Topo Maps: Orange County topo or USGS 7.5 minute series (Alberhill)
Campgrounds/Facilities: Blue Jay Camp / El Cariso Ranger Station
Nearest Services: San Juan Capistrano

Getting There: Take I-5 to San Juan Capistrano and take the 74 Freeway east 22 miles to El Cariso. Just beyond the east edge of the village is the El Cariso Ranger Station, and 1,000 feet east of the station is the entrance to 3S04, the South Main Divide Truck Trail. Turn left and park your car conveniently. If you're a neophyte and just want to test yourself with six miles, you could have someone drive a vehicle to Blue Jay Camp to meet you.

Head north on 3S04. The road meanders atop the eastern escarpment of the Santa Ana Mountains (above Temescal Valley), and there are many viewing areas along the way where you can see the San Bernardino, San Gabriel, and San Jacinto mountains. Snowcapped on a clear winter day, these peaks are impressive. Riding along the twisting road you also look over chaparral-covered hills and forested valleys. At 5.3 miles, the road forks. Take the left fork that drops into a series of wide, golden meadows. (The right fork goes farther up into the mountains.) One mile after the road forks you enter Blue Jay Camp. The area is covered with oaks bordering the beautiful meadow lands. There is water here, as well as picnic tables and restrooms, the ideal spot to rest before returning to your car.

#2 South Main Divide Trail to Santiago Peak and Return

Mileage: 23 miles round trip from the gated area above Blue Jay Camp
Water: Blue Jay Camp
Level of Difficulty: Difficult
Elevation: Begin 3,600+ feet. High point: 5,687 feet. End: 3,600+ feet.
Topo Maps: Orange County topo or USGS 7.5 minute series (Alberhill, Santiago Peak)
Campgrounds/Facilities: Blue Jay Camp
Nearest Services: San Juan Capistrano

Getting There: Follow the directions in Ride #1 to the Main Divide Truck Trail. Drive up the trail 5.5 miles to fork. The left branch goes down into Blue Jay Camp (1 mile). The right branch ends in about 100 yards at a gate. (I park my vehicle where the two roads diverge. Lots of easy parking there.) Pedal past the gate onto the dirt road and put your climbin' shoes on.

The trail (3S04) continues on a hillside of grass and brush. For 1.5 miles and over 600 feet of elevation gain, the ridges stay that way. Suddenly a forest of pine trees appears next to a group of metal barricades. Off to the left is Mt. Piños on a high grassy ridge dotted with pines.

Curves right past the barricades and pines the road alternately rises and drops until you reach the junction of the Indian Truck Trail (5S01) about 7 miles along. The ridges where the Main Divide Trail runs are dominated by brush and small trees. Excellent views to the east include mountain and lowland areas.

From the Indian Truck Trail Junction, keep on 3S04. You climb a lot: in 4 miles you ascend 1,900 feet up a series of slippery, unstable, rock piles (called a road) to the top of Santiago Peak. On a clear day the view from Santiago Peak is breathtaking. Enjoy the view, you've earned it (as well as a coronary).

On the return trip you ride off the mountain top and turn right at the divided road. This points you toward your car. The descent is brutal so be careful. (I've dumped my bike at least twice on the way down.)

Once you've made your final elevation gains, the trip back along the Main Divide Road (high above Riverside County) is especially enjoyable. There's lots to see on the eastern slope of the Santa Anas. The San Bernardino and San Jacinto mountains stand in the distance. See the Temescal Valley below and the growing community of Elsinore (with lake attached). The lowlands of Riverside County stretch to the horizon. The Main Divide Trail finally emerges on the western slope of the Santa Anas. All around is the remote ruggedness of this part of the National Forest.

The final one-mile drop to your car is a real "white knuckler," complete with eroded trail sections big enough to swallow a truck. An added advantage of this portion of the Main Divide Trail is that there are fewer riders than farther north, and trail usage is also much lighter than on either the Silverado or Modjeska trails.

#3 South Main Divide Trail to Indian Truck Trail – Car Shuttle
Mileage: 13 miles
Water: Blue Jay Camp
Level of Difficulty: Difficult, moderate
Elevation: Begin 3,600+ feet. High point: 4,400+ feet. End: 1,200+ feet.
Topo Maps: Orange County topo or USGS 7.5 minute series (Alberhill, Santiago Peak)
Campgrounds/Facilities: Blue Jay Camp, 1 miles south of gated end of 3S04
Nearest Services: San Juan Capistrano

Parking Your Second Car: Take the 91 Freeway east. Drive past Corona to I-15. Go south 7 miles to the Indian Truck Trail turnoff. Turn right from the off ramp. The Indian Truck Trail becomes a dirt road. Travel 0.5 miles to a fork. Turn left at the sign and drive another 1.6 miles to the trailhead (just past the religious center). Park 80 yards below the Forest Service gate.

As in Ride #2, drive to El Cariso and up the Main Divide Truck Trail to the gate just above Blue Jay Camp. Ride on 3S04, climbing sharply and immediately to Los Piños Saddle. (There you'll find a large stand of pine trees and some metal pipe barricades.) The chaparral of the lower trail has given way to a small pine forest. The high ridge southwest of the road is part of Mt. Piños. Conifers dot the mountainside. Continue to the right, downhill past the pines where you begin a series of moderate elevation gains and losses.

All along this part of the Main Divide are many viewing areas. Directly east of the road the eastern escarpment of the Santa Anas is filled with steep canyons and mountainsides dropping sharply to the plain below. To the south is Lake Elsinore and much more.

After 7.5 miles you reach the Indian Truck Trail (5S01). Turn right. This trail twists and turns along ridge lines down into the Temescal Valley at the foot of the Santa Ana Mountains. You'll find the road relatively clean and thus fast-paced to the bottom.

Just down the road a little way from the Indian Truck Trail gate is a Korean religious retreat center. Respect this place of contemplation and silence. As life would have it, just off the property boundary you'll notice that every road sign is bullet-riddled amidst piles of spent shell casings.

Photo: Steve Giberson

CHAPTER 6

TRABUCO CANYON

Encamped near this canyon in 1769 a group of Spanish soldiers were sent to search the area on an important mission. One of the accompanying cavalry soldiers lost his rifle, called a *trabuco,* and never found it. A lost firearm—an item representing the balance of power over a sullen populace—was something to fear for an occupying army. The memory of their fruitless search has come down to us in the name Trabuco Canyon.

The Mission Fathers took possession of the land, running cattle to the south of the canyon on a wide plain called *Plano Trabuco.* Later, with Mexico's independence from Spain, the missions were disbanded and the lands redistributed. California's governor gave this canyon as part of a 22,000-acre land grant to Santiago Arguello in 1841. Thus were many of the great *ranchos* of California created.

In Indian times, Trabuco Canyon was part of a trail that crossed the Santa Ana Mountains into Riverside County. Later the trail was used by horse thieves escaping Orange County with stolen stock. The connecting trail out of Trabuco Canyon is today called "Horse Thief Trail."

As you ride through Trabuco, you will enjoy its waters and its lushness. Farther up the mountain you'll find mixed pine forests, dark and cool, as you make your long, steady climb to the high ridges.

#1   South Main Divide Trail to Trabuco Canyon
Mileage: 6.5 miles one way to Holy Jim Canyon, 13 miles round trip to Holy Jim and return, or 11 miles one way to the beginning of Trabuco Canyon
Water: Blue Jay Camp
Level of Difficulty: Moderate
Elevation: Begin: 3,600+ feet. High point: 4,190+ feet. Low point: 1,000+ feet.
Topo Maps: Orange County topo or USGS 7.5 minute series (Alberhill, Santiago Peak)
Campgrounds/Facilities: Blue Jay Camp
Nearest Services: San Juan Capistrano and Mission Viejo

Getting There: Follow the directions in Ride #1, Chapter 5.

Parking Your Second Car: Take I-5 to Mission Viejo. Exit on El Toro Road and head 7.6 miles east to where the road forks. Go right onto Live Oak Canyon Road (S19). Approximately 2 miles later you pass O'Neill Regional Park and find an open creek bed to your left. A dirt road enters the creek's flood plain area. This is the entrance to Trabuco Canyon. If your car has a low ground clearance, park at the canyon entrance. Otherwise, proceed up the bumpy, rocky road to Holy Jim Canyon Firehouse (4.5 miles) at the mouth of Holy Jim Canyon, where there is good parking.

Begin your ride from the gated Main Divide Trail (3S04) about 1 mile above Blue Jay Camp. You'll see a cluster of metal pipe barricades at a "cul-de-sac" about 1.5 miles up the trail. At these barricades follow 3S04 to the right. Roll downhill 10 to 20 yards looking for a small trail post in some trees on your left. Turn left onto Trabuco Trail (6W04) and prepare yourself for a wonderful ride through dark forest glens. The air is cool in the shade of oak and pine trees. Small trees and brush form canopies over the trail like "Hobbit" tunnels. Enjoy more technical riding, too. Halfway down the canyon the trail becomes a boulder slalom of spine-jarring proportions. At the bottom of Trabuco Trail, 2.5 miles from the Los Piños Saddle, you intersect with the West Horse Thief Trail (6W11). Turn left along Trabuco Creek beneath large oak and sycamore trees. Ride 2 miles to Holy Jim Canyon for a total of 6.5 miles.

If you parked a second car at the head of Trabuco Canyon, continue west from the Holy Jim Fire Station 4.5 more miles along the Trabuco Canyon dirt road (6S13). This portion of the trip is relatively flat and very mellow. Be careful to stay on the dirt road and not to wander off onto the posted private property.

If you didn't drop a second vehicle, you'll be retracing your route back to the Main Divide Truck Trail above Blue Jay Camp. Take a rest at Holy Jim Canyon before heading back up Trabuco Trail, which is quite rocky for a while. However, halfway up Trabuco Trail the ground becomes smoother for long, steady climbing, and you'll make good progress to the junction with the Main Divide (3S04). From Los Piños Saddle, the exit of Trabuco Trail, turn right on 3S04 and it's all downhill to your car. Total mileage round trip is 13 miles.

#2   Trabuco Canyon Road to Holy Jim Canyon and Return

Mileage: 9 miles round trip
Level of Difficulty: Beginner
Elevation: Begin: 1,100+ feet. High point 1,700+ feet. End: 1,100+ feet.
Topo Maps: Orange County topo or USGS 7.5 minute series (Santiago Peak)
Campgrounds/Facilities: None
Nearest Services: Mission Viejo

Getting There: See "Parking Your Second Car" in Ride #1, this chapter, and park at the beginning of Trabuco Canyon Road.

Ride up Trabuco Canyon Road, which at first is rocky with a gradual climb as you leave the lower canyon and head up into the National Forest. Oaks and sycamores grow tall along Trabuco Creek and there can be many wet stream crossings depending on the season. In the absence of vehicle traffic this can be a pleasant ride. In 4.5 miles you come to Holy Jim Fire Station, a good rest spot before returning to your car. Taken slowly, this is a great starter trail for the new mountain biker.

CHAPTER 7

A ONE TRACK MIND:
SINGLE TRACKS OF THE SANTA ANAS

There are those mountain bikers who seek out the single track experience. They prefer riding rugged hiking trails instead of dirt roads, and the nastier the better. Fortunately, for the seriders, the Cleveland National Forest contains numerous challenging trails. If self-punishment is what you seek, read on. Single track trails require extra precautions from you, the rider. Watch your speed! Extra inner tubes are a must, as is a bike repair kit and first-aid kit. Long pants and shirt are needed to protect you from the brush along the trail. They will keep you from unnecessary cuts and scratches as well as tick infestation.

#1 San Juan Trail (6W05) to Blue Jay Camp and Return

Mileage: 22 miles
Water: Blue Jay Camp
Level of Difficulty: Intermediate, difficult
Elevations: Begin: 800+ feet. High point: 3,300+ feet. End: 800+ feet.
Topo Maps: Orange County topo or USGS 7.5 minute series (Cañada Gobernadora, Alberhill)
Campgrounds: Blue Jay Camp
Nearest Services: San Juan Capistrano

Getting There: Take I-5 to San Juan Capistrano. Exit on Highway 74, and drive east 12.5 miles. You'll see a sign for San Juan Hot Springs and you will notice some Forest Service buildings. Turn left here and drive down the canyon 1 mile to the trailhead. (There is plenty of parking in a grove of trees to the left.)

The trail begins as a series of switchbacks going straight up the mountainside. Daunting as it looks, the trail is well-engineered and the grades are within the abilities of "mere mortals."

Approximately 3 to 4 miles from the entrance of the trail you begin passing high ridges and mountain tops. The great valleys lie here and there. You see Highway 74 as a tiny line stretched across the mountains. The climb is sometimes steep and other times gradual, but always relentless to 3,000+ feet. I caution you to take the greatest care when you ride this route, especially on the down side. Every gnarly rock, root, and pitfall imaginable exists on this wonderful trail. You'll note the path has lots of foot traffic, especially on weekends.

At mile 5.4, the trail forks with an eroded old road (Route A) to the left and a continuation of the footpath (Route B) is to the right. Both paths wind up at Blue Jay Camp.

Route A: At the San Juan Trail junction bear left on the deteriorated road. Follow this about 4 miles to a meadow area. You'll cross over another path and climb steeply up a hill. (The soil is rocky and unstable.) Near the top of the hill you'll find another footpath. Turn right. Ride a mile or so to Blue Jay Camp.

Route B: At the San Juan Trail junction bear right. After you ride along the footpath to mile 9, you will a see another trail on your right. This is the Chiquito Trail. Continue past it, bearing left on a path skirting the bottom of a hill. At the bottom of a hill you cross over an old road and take the gentle switchbacks up the hill to Blue Jay Camp. The camp area, which affords shade and usually has water, is a great spot to rest before your return.

The trip back is a riot. At the end of the ride you have an optional hot tub soak at San Juan Hot Springs. How thoughtful!

#2   Los Piños Trail (6W06)
Mileage: 18 miles round trip
Water: None
Level of Difficulty: Difficult, experts only
Elevation: Begin: 900+ feet. High point: 4,510 feet. End: 900+ feet.
Topo Maps: Orange County topo or USGS 7.5 minute series (Cañada Gobernadora, Santiago Peak, Alberhill)
Campgrounds: None
Nearest Services: San Juan Capistrano

Getting There: Follow driving and parking instructions for Ride #1.

From the San Juan trailhead ride 0.5 miles north into the canyon to the gate of the Lazy W Ranch. (This is a private camp leased by religious

organizations for church functions.) Entering the camp you see two roads: one left (past a gate) and one right. Pass to the right. You must ask permission at the office to cross 200 yards or so of private land. Then go back to the left road to find the public trail (6406). (Camp workmen have usually just waved me on. You may not park on ranch land.) From the metal gate ride about 200 yards to a trailhead beginning with some steps to your left. Walk your bike over the steps and begin riding uphill. The trail changes from O.K. to gruesome, shortly. Unstable soil, rocky and vertical conditions all combine to make a tough climb. Two miles or so up the trail conditions improve a bit as the trail evolves into a firebreak. From there you climb steadily all the way to Mount Piños (4,510 feet).

The high ridges and peaks along the Los Piños Trail are among the most isolated of the Santa Ana Mountains. Numerous rugged valleys lie scattered below you while Saddleback Mountain looms high to the east. The foothills of the Santa Ana Mountains descend slowly to the west, all providing a great view.

You must struggle with the toughest of conditions to the top of Mt. Piños and back. The trail is severely eroded in places. Be cautious the entire distance. Like a challenge? This is it. Downhill is no less formidable as you ride for home. You will undoubtedly want to walk your bike at certain "special" sections of the trail (rather than maim yourself).

#3   Chiquito Trail (6407) / San Juan Loop (5408)
Mileage: 18.6 miles round trip
Water: None
Level of Difficulty: Difficult, intermediate
Elevation: Begin: 1,700+ feet. High point: 2,800+ feet. End: 1,700+ feet.
Topo Maps: Orange County topo or USGS 7.5 minute series (Sitton Peak, Alberhill)
Campgrounds: Blue Jay Camp
Nearest Services: San Juan Capistrano

Getting There: Take I-5 and exit onto Highway 74 at San Juan Capistrano. Drive 19 miles east. You'll see a small store on the right; park in the lot on the left.

You have the choice of circling north (right) or south (left) from the parking lot on the San Juan Loop Trail, 5408. Either route will take you to the Chiquito Trail 1 mile from the parking lot.

Note that the Chiquito Trail (6407) follows a small stream heading north back into a canyon. You ride another mile along the trail or in the stream bed (usually dry) before the trail rises up the ridge and becomes quite difficult in places. Expert riders should have no trouble muscling their way through these tough spots.

Near the top of the ridge line follow the trail around the ridge into Lion Canyon. Your best riding starts here. The trails are wide and relatively free of debris. The ascent up the valley is gradual compared to the ridge climb. Enjoy the valley itself, a shaded, grassy woodland. It's cool and comfortable. At the valley's end you see a saddle bordered by several minor hilltops. Cresting the saddle bend you reach a small meadow with markers for the upper entrance of Chiquito Trail (6407), which marks the turnaround point for this ride.

Retrace your route to the San Juan Loop below. At the loop, the right fork is probably the best way back to the parking lot. You've made an exhausting, though enjoyable ride.

Comments: Directly across the parking lot from the San Juan Loop you'll find "a cold one." Not only does this mini-market stock the usual, it carries a great selection of homemade candies. Many's the time I hated myself after a visit there. Candy designated for "the family" never made it home. Anyway, the "Candy Store" is a culinary tradition with hikers and locals.

Lion Canyon: Lion Canyon is the area through which Chiquito Trail passes. After winter rains, the lush greenery here reminds me of Hansel and Gretel's forest. My 8-year-old daughter thought it was "tropical." Since the rider is usually surrounded by chaparral in these parts, it's a nice change of pace.

#4 Trabuco Trail (6404) / West Horse Thief Trail (5401)

Mileage: 11.5 miles round trip
Water: None
Level of Difficulty: Intermediate, difficult
Elevation: Begin: 1,900+ feet. High point: 4,200+ feet. End: 1,900+ feet.
Topo Maps: Orange County topo or USGS 7.5 minute series (Santiago Peak, Alberhill)
Campgrounds: None
Nearest Services: Mission Viejo

Getting There: See "Parking Your Second Car" in Ride #1, Chapter 6.

Provided your vehicle has adequate clearance, drive up Trabuco Canyon and park your car 1 mile beyond Holy Jim Canyon at road's end (plenty of parking). Ride the rocky trail 1.8 miles to the junction of West Horse Thief Trail and Trabuco Trail. Take the right fork, which is much better for uphill travel than the West Horse Thief Trail. The Horse Thief Trail is too steep and the soil conditions make riding very difficult.

The lower portion of the Trabuco Trail is very rocky. You ascend a small canyon and enter some of the lushest woodlands in the Santa Ana Mountains. Large bushes grow over the trail in many areas forming "Hobbit Tunnels" for you to glide through in the gloom of the darkened forest. The trails improve substantially for bike riding the higher you climb toward Los Piños saddle and the Main Divide Truck Trail. You emerge from the forest onto 3S04 at Los Piños Saddle, 2.7 miles from the lower trail junction on Trabuco Creek. Turn left. In 3 miles of elevation gains and losses you find the West Horse Thief Trail (5401) on your left which begins as a firebreak and becomes a footpath. At 1.9 miles down the mountain you struggle with an unending series of switchbacks, twisting and sliding on unstable shale soil. You might ask yourself, "Am I riding or skiing?" and you answer "Both" until you finally reach the valley bottom linking you with Trabuco Canyon Trail. From here you have a serene ride back to your car at the end of Trabuco Road.

#5   Joplin Trail (6W02) via Santiago Truck Trail and Return

Mileage: 20.4 round trip
Water: None
Level of Difficulty: Moderate, difficult
Elevation: Begin: 1,500 feet. High point: 4,900 feet. End: 1,500 feet.
Topo Maps: Orange County topo or USGS 7.5 minute series (Santiago Peak)
Campgrounds: None
Nearest Services: Mission Viejo / Silverado Canyon

Getting There: From Orange and the 55 Freeway, go east on Chapman, which becomes Santiago Canyon Road. Drive 14.1 miles to Modjeska Grade Road and turn left. In about 1/2 mile you reach a metal pipe gate beneath several power line towers.

From the Mission Viejo area take I- 5 to El Toro Road and head east 7.6 miles to where the road forks. Turn left onto Santiago Canyon Road. Drive 0.9 more miles to Modjeska Grade Road and turn right. Proceed about 1/2 mile to the steel gate beneath the power lines.

Pass the metal gate and ride the Santiago Truck Trail 7.5 miles through the hills. The road snakes its way around the contours of the land past some of Orange County's most eye-catching rock formations. At about mile 5.5 you'll see a road dropping sharply to the right off the Santiago Trail. This is the Joplin Road (not trail), which dead-ends several hundred feet below Santiago Trail. Pass it by; there's no exit.

Two miles later you reach a fork in the road. The right fork dead-ends after about a mile. Take the left fork, and the road drops into a small river valley. This valley is the site of Old Camp, reputedly an ancient hunting camp used by local Indians. Follow the road into a small clearing. Look across the clearing (left) to an opposite hillside. (The hillside is part of a valley dropping into Old Camp from above.) Find and take a small footpath (there are no signs) that leads you up the valley 2.2 miles to the Main Divide Truck Trail (3S04).

The path is steep. Expert riders will streak upwards to the amazement and shame of the rest of us. Intermediate riders will "walk n' ride" steadily to the top. Large sections of the trail are well done, however, enabling you to realistically bike most of the distance.

Not only is Joplin Trail beautiful, but you'll be pleased to note that few people use it. The day you ride there it will probably be your own private park. Returning to your car from the top of Joplin Trail is its own reward. You will bob, weave, brake and slide down this entire narrow ribbon of trail. Joplin Trail is "E ticket" riding material all the way. On completing the trip down, the only question in your mind will be, "When do we come back?"

On the Santiago Truck Trail from Old Camp, return 7.7 miles to your car.

Photo: Steve Giberson

CHAPTER 8

GETTING DOWN: ORANGE COUNTY SINGLE TRACKS FROM TOP TO BOTTOM

A good backpacking friend of mine has a peculiar preference. He would always choose going downhill over up. So much so he'd even trudge up a mountain just for the pleasure of going down the other side.

It is in this spirit that I offer you the opportunity to experience Orange County's toughest trails from the top down. Simple car shuttle arrangements make it possible for you to do two or more of these strenuous trails in a day. Does that make the trails easy? No. There is enough treacherous terrain here to claim you many times over. Going downhill merely increases the speed by which you might wrack up your bike and body.

There are several things to consider when taking these trails downhill:
• These are all difficult rides. Don't get in over your head.
• Speed: Keep it down. Good sense and safety demands it. After several downhill runs on a trail, you'll be able to develop quicker times.
• Tire pressure: High (35-40 lbs.). The rocks are brutal, and low inflation means bent wheel rims and money down the drain.
• Watch out for hikers. If you want to continue to ride here, you must respect and protect them.
• Lower your seat: A lower saddle means a better center of gravity for going downhill. Perching up high, as you would ride on flat ground, will send you over your handle bars when you go down steep grades.

#1   San Juan Trail Car Shuttle (6W05)
Blue Jay Camp to Hot Springs Canyon (San Juan Trail): 11 miles
Topo Maps: Orange County topo or USGS 7.5 minute series (Alberhill, Sitton Peak, Cañada Gobernadora)
Parking: See Ride #2, Chapter 5 and Ride #1, Chapter 7

San Juan Trail is pure fun. It is the fastest of all the National Forest trails but still packed full of challenging obstacles. A word of caution: Two people have been rescued on this trail in recent months (fall 1992). Ride carefully and responsibly!

Begin at the southern end of Blue Jay Camp, where you'll find a posted trailhead leading out across the hills. A mile or so from the trailhead you'll see an eroded trail rising steeply to meet the path you're on. This is one part of 6W05, the San Juan Trail. Turn left. If you prefer, you can pass this trail junction and continue along the hillside contours descending more gently to a valley below. This track crosses an eroded path and then heads up into some hills toward Hot Springs Canyon. You'll merge with the eroded path again, continuing down the San Juan Trail. (Both the eroded path and your trail are part of San Juan Trail.) Continue on to your second car at Hot Springs Canyon.

#2 Chiquito Trail (6W07) Car Shuttle

From Blue Jay Camp to San Juan Loop parking lot: 10 miles
Topo Maps: Orange County topo or USGS 7.5 minute series (Alberhill, Sitton Peak)
Parking: See Ride #2, Chapter 5 and Ride #3, Chapter 7

Begin at the southern end of Blue Jay Camp, where you'll find a posted trailhead leading out across the hills. Approximately 1 mile from the trailhead you'll see an eroded trail rising steeply to intersect the path you're on. Continue on the footpath as it follows the hillside and you see signs for Chiquito Trail. From the Chiquito trailhead, you drop sharply into Lion Canyon. Here you'll ride wide, clean trails that take you out of the canyon and around the end of a ridge line. The trail drops roughly as you ride down the opposite slope of the ridge line finally into a river valley.

Follow the trail and creek bed another mile or so until you intersect the San Juan Loop Trail (5W08). You can go either left or right around the loop to reach your second car. Then you are across Highway 74 from the "Candy Store." It's time for some decadence.

#3 Los Piños Trail Car Shuttle

From 3S04 above Blue Jay Camp to San Juan Trail parking lot in Hot Springs Canyon: 11 miles
For experts only: this is probably the toughest trail in the Santa Anas
Topo Maps: Orange County topo or USGS 7.5 minute series (Alberhill, Santiago Peak, Cañada Gobernadora)
Parking: See Ride #2, Chapter 5 and Ride #1, Chapter 7

Ride your bike past the metal gate on 3S04, 1 mile above Blue Jay Camp. Climb steeply into the hills 1 mile past the gate. The grade will flatten out and you'll find yourself at a "cul-de-sac" in the road surrounded by metal barriers.

Take your bike over the barriers and around the right side of a steep hill. This is the trail to Mt. Piños. Follow the trail along the ridge line toward the peak. The trail from the peak of Mt. Piños is a wide firebreak. It rises and falls along a ridge line several miles until it turns left toward Hot Springs Canyon. Follow this combination trail/firebreak down to Hot Springs Canyon. As mentioned earlier, long pants and long sleeves will help you from being too scratched up by brush and thorn along the trail. Carry lots of water. Warm weather travel here is not recommended.

When you reach the bottom of Los Piños Trail, ride your bike about 1 mile to the San Juan Loop parking area to pick up your second car.

#4 Joplin Trail / Santiago Truck Trail Car Shuttle

Starting points and mileages vary (see below)
Topo Maps: Orange County topo or USGS 7.5 minute series (Alberhill, Sitton Peak, Cañada Gobernadora)
Parking Your Second Car: See Ride #7, Chapter 4

As mentioned in the previous chapter, Joplin Trail is a thrilling downhill run. It begins from the Main Divide Truck Trail (3S04) at 4,900 feet and drops 3,000 feet in the space of 2.2 miles. The trail ends at "Old Camp" 7.7 miles from Modjeska Grade Road, your eventual exit and second car drop. There are three approaches to Joplin Trail as described in A, B, and C below.

(A) From Maple Spring Trail: 19.2 miles
From Silverado Canyon enter the metal gate onto Maple Spring Road (see Ride #2, Chapter 3). Ride 7 miles up the mountain to the four-way trail junction. Go up the incline and make a right turn (3S04). Continue toward Saddleback Mountain another 2.3 miles. You must look carefully to your right to locate the Joplin trailhead (no trailside signs). Take a right turn off onto the trail and the fun begins.

(B) From Silverado Canyon Road: 12.2 miles (auto shuttle to the top)
See Ride #2, Chapter 3, to reach the gate in Silverado Canyon. If the gate is open, continue driving uphill 7 miles and park your car near the four-way trail junction of Maple Spring Trail, Harding Truck Trail and north and south Main Divide Trail. The advantage? Physically, you're fresh at the beginning of the downhill. Ride 2.3 miles along 3S04 toward Saddleback Mountain and turn right on Joplin Trail. The rest of the ride is predominantly descending (almost 10 miles). Isn't that every rider's dream—a "free lunch"?

Photo: Robert Rasmussen

(C) From Modjeska Canyon: 21.5 miles

Depart from the Tucker Wildlife area via Harding Truck Trail #5S08 (see Ride #1, Chapter 4). Biking up Harding Trail you reach the four-way trail junction after 9.3 miles. With two quick right turns you are on the Main Divide Truck Trail (3S04) headed toward Santiago Peak. You reach Joplin Trail in about 2.3 miles. Keep looking to the right down the steep mountainside to find the trail opening and turn right. The downhill sure is fun, but not if you hurt yourself. Please ride responsibly.

Note: The winter day I rode the Joplin Trail, soil conditions were unstable, causing my machine to skid this way and that. It was like "Nintendo" for your bike: quick reactions, fast corrections, and a challenging ride.

A winter storm was closing fast upon the Saddleback Mountain area. The upper reaches of the peaks were covered in misty gray clouds, making them invisible from the lowlands. From on high, everything was socked in, allowing only hundred-yard visibility down the mountain. As I pointed my bike down the narrow ribbon of trail, the path quickly disappeared into the mist. Gaining speed downhill was like parachuting into the clouds and wondering what there was on the other side.

Several hundred feet lower, the cloud cap broke, revealing the full valley—chaparral, meadow lands, and thick forest. Because of the foggy conditions, all plant colors were especially vibrant, almost electrical, much brighter than usual. Ahead of me on the trail I saw a lone bike track in the moist earth, fresh; a day, perhaps a few hours old. Then I began to notice another track, fresher still. About the size of a man's fist, it was not the print of a hoofed animal, but rather one with claws tucked in—obviously a large cat. Its tracks wandered along the path for a mile or so. I wondered if the animal had been stalking the other rider or simply walking on the trail. Since I was riding alone, I began to look over my shoulder a lot and imagine things. It was time to make tracks of my own!

Eventually I found Old Camp, which makes a great rest spot under ancient towering oaks. From there it's a short hop to Santiago Trail and the final leg of the journey.

If you like to bike and love the mountains, you can't help but enjoy the Joplin Trail.

CHAPTER 9

CASPERS PARK AND SAN JUAN HOT SPRINGS

In 1769 Don Gaspar de Portola entered Orange County with his Spanish troops for the first time. Six years later, a second expedition was sent from Mission San Diego to form a permanent mission outpost. The site chosen was located along present-day San Juan Creek, a couple of miles south of Caspers Park. The new mission was soon abandoned, however. The Spanish were shocked to learn that the San Diego Mission had just been burned to the ground by its recent Indian converts. The military contingent on San Juan Creek picked up and went south immediately to halt the rebellion.

One year later, the Spaniards returned but relocated the Mission site to San Juan Capistrano. Mission friars ran their herds of cattle throughout the Caspers Park area. Later when the missions disbanded, much land speculation occurred. Modern-day Caspers Park was absorbed into Rancho Santa Margarita, a 226,000-acre domain spread over three counties.

In the 1960s and 1970s, members of the Orange County Board of Supervisors were concerned that rampant development would soon leave nothing to enjoy of Orange County's backcountry. Ronald W. Caspers, a prominent Board member, was a prime mover in the struggle to buy and preserve rural Orange County land for future citizens. Caspers Park was named after him upon his death in 1974.

Caspers Park is a microcosm of the natural beauty found throughout Orange County. Shaded forest glens, grasslands, creeks, high steep ridges—all are here to be enjoyed. Mountain bikes may be used only on dirt roads. Single-track riding is forbidden here due to large numbers of hikers.

Visiting Caspers Park over the years I've seen rabbits, deer, coyotes, vultures, hawks, quail, and on one occasion a mountain lion. In fact, two mountain lion attacks in the late 1980s have forced County authorities to forbid entry to minors in the park, so you may not bring your children.

Caspers Park

Mileage: Over 25 miles of trails
Water: At restrooms and picnic/camp sites
Level of Difficulty: Beginner and intermediate
Topo Maps: Orange County topo or USGS 7.5 minute series (Cañada Gobernadora)
Camping: Throughout the park; see rangers for details
Nearest Services: San Juan Capistrano, 7.5 miles

Getting There: Take I-5 to San Juan Capistrano. Exit on Highway 74 east (Ortega Highway). Drive 7.5 miles east on winding mountain roads until you see the sign for Caspers Park. Turn left and enter the park. For the San Juan Hot Springs ride you drive approximately 5 miles east of the Caspers Park entrance.

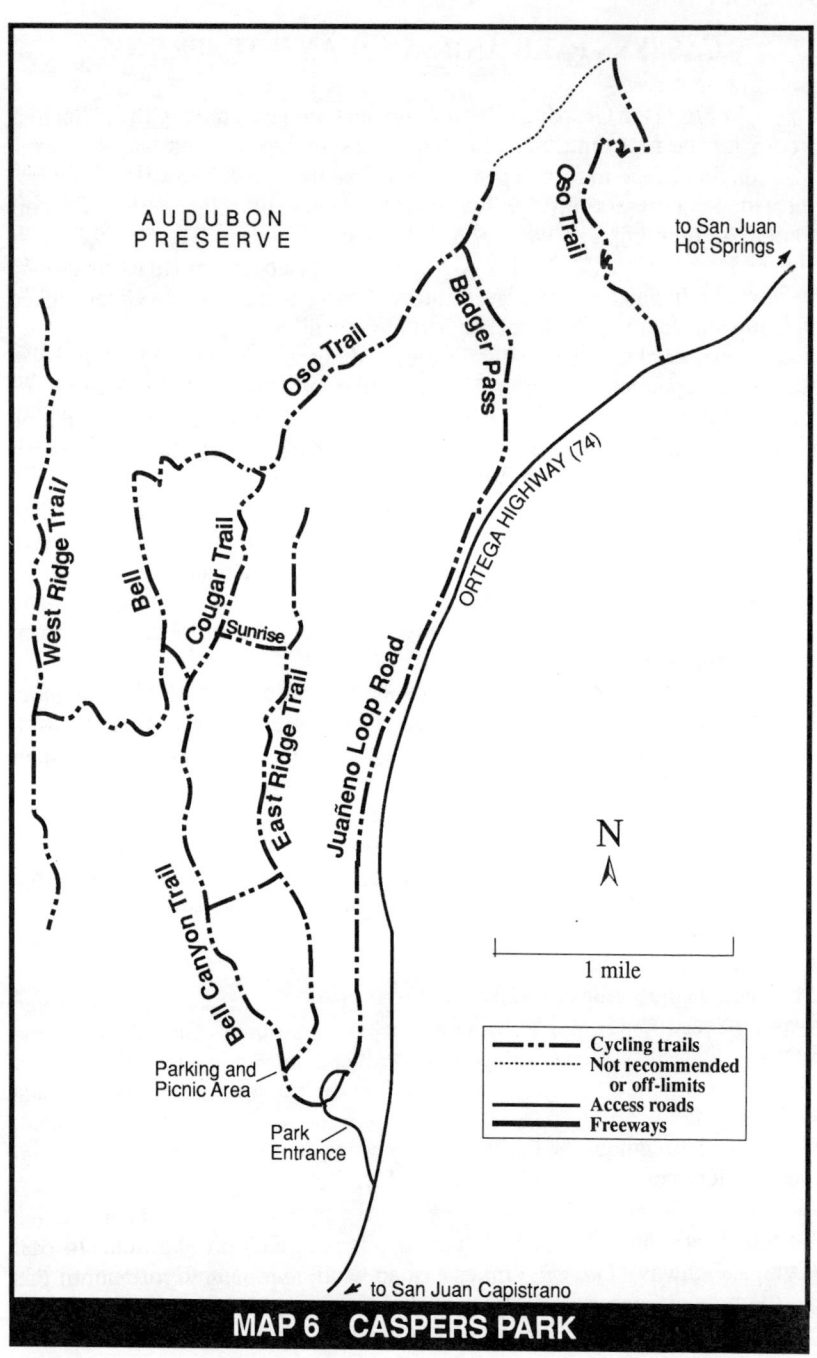

AUDUBON
PRESERVE

Oso Trail

to San Juan
Hot Springs

Oso Trail

Badger Pass

ORTEGA HIGHWAY (74)

West Ridge Trail

Bell

Cougar Trail

Sunrise

East Ridge Trail

Juañeno Loop Road

Bell Canyon Trail

N

1 mile

Parking and
Picnic Area

Park
Entrance

Cycling trails
Not recommended
or off-limits
Access roads
Freeways

to San Juan Capistrano

MAP 6   CASPERS PARK

#1 Bell Canyon Trail

Miles: 4.4 miles round trip
Water: Restroom and picnic/camping areas
Level of Difficulty: Beginner
Elevation: Begin: 400+ feet. High point: 600 feet. End: 400+ feet.

Enter Caspers Park, following the blacktop past horse and camping areas about 1 mile to the end of the road. Park your car. You will find a dirt road with a gate. Ride down this road 1 mile through lovely meadows, tall oaks, and assorted grasslands. You will come to a junction posted *Cougar Pass to the right*. Bear left, continuing on Bell Canyon Road another 1.2 miles to the end of the road. Turn around and return to your car.

The area near the end of Bell Canyon Road is delightful, with tall and gnarled oaks. The grass beneath them is lushly green and inviting at the beginning of spring. It's a great spot to take a rest or make a romantic picnic under the trees. One word of caution: The closed-off road at the end of the park marks the border of Starr Ranch, a nature conservancy of the Audubon Society. Many scientific studies are done here. Please do not enter the Audubon area.

#2 East Ridge Loop

Mile: 5.2 round trip
Water: Restroom and camping/picnic areas only
Level of Difficulty: Beginner, intermediate
Elevation: Begin: 400+ feet. High point: 900+ feet. End: 400+ feet.

Drive into Caspers Park, cross the river bed and go up a small hill bearing right at a "Y" intersection. A few yards up the road you'll see a dirt road with a gate. Park your car just off the main black top road in the first available spot. (Watch the parking signs.)

Take your bike past the gate. You now begin a long, gradual 500-foot climb up the east ridge of Caspers Park. If you stop to look out over the ridge line toward Ortega Highway, you'll note that the ridge drops sharply as you continue up the road, becoming a very sheer cliff. (Since the soil is unstable, stay back from the edge by a few feet.)

Half-way up the ridge road, look to your left where you'll notice a large grassy plain with some stunted trees that bear a striking resemblance to the "savannah" or grasslands of East Africa. After 2 miles you pass an extremely steep road dropping off to your left toward Bell Canyon. This connector road is called Sunrise, and because of its steepness, beginners should not use it.

At 2.5 miles the East Ridge trail ends. A small lookout path to the right can be taken (great views of the surrounding countryside), or you can bear to the left and take an unnamed connector road down the ridge. You come to the Cougar Pass connector trail. Turn left on Cougar and drop 0.5 miles to Bell Canyon Road. Follow Bell Canyon Road to the blacktop. Continue on this asphalt road through the picnic and horse camp areas for 1 mile until you reach your car at the beginning of East Ridge Trail.

#3 Juaneño Loop
Miles: 8.3 miles
Water: Restrooms and camping/picnic sites only
Level of Difficulty: Intermediate
Elevation: Begin: 400+ feet. High point: 1,400+ feet. End: 400+ feet.

Enter Caspers Park and park your car to the right of the ranger station. Near the bridge over the creek, find and begin riding on a dirt road heading north below the East Ridge. The road becomes a firebreak that runs parallel with the Ortega Highway.

You will come to a creek crossing; above and to your right a highway bridge spans the creek. Cross to the other side, following the firebreak until it veers left and begins leading steeply uphill toward the distant ridge line (Badger Pass). You are on Badger Pass Trail, and much of it is a walk-up due to steepness and bad soil conditions. It reaches the top of the ridge quickly, however, and you find a welcome rest area.

At the rest area, Oso Trail comes up from below to intersect with Badger Pass. A right turn takes you farther into the backcountry to a dead end overlooking Starr Ranch. No bicycles allowed into the ranch.

Take the left turn from Badger Pass down Oso Trail, beginning a steep dive toward the connector trail, Cougar Pass. Turn on to Cougar Pass Trail and continue into Bell Canyon, connecting with Bell Canyon Trail to return to the picnic/horse camp area. Follow the asphalt road through the park down toward the entrance station and return to your car.

Due to the elevation gain of this ride, it is probably the most scenic excursion in the park. For miles you can look up and down several canyon areas and rugged mountain ridges. There are variations on this trip, if you wish to pass on the Juaneño firebreak (it's a junky road surface). I've gone up and down the Badger Pass Trail and can assure you the descent is hair-raising. I dumped my bike several times and urge you to exercise the utmost caution.

#4 West Ridge Trail
Miles: 4.9 miles
Water: Restrooms and camping/picnic sites only
Level of Difficulty: Beginner
Elevation: Begin: 400+ feet. High point: 800+ feet. End: 400+ feet.

From the park entrance follow the asphalt road across the creek bed, up the hill, and turn right at the stop sign. Continue on the asphalt road through the horse and picnic areas to where it dead-ends.

From the parking area, ride on the dirt road and pass the metal gate. Ride 1.2 miles to the junction of Cougar Pass intersecting Bell Canyon Road from the right. At this junction, bear left for a few yards and find another dirt road intersecting Bell Canyon Road from your left. Turn left. Follow this unmarked road 0.2 miles to Star Rise, a dirt road heading up to the top of the West Ridge.

As you crest the West Ridge, the bike trail runs both right and left for a total of 2.2 miles. The views are excellent. Rugged ridges and river valleys abound. You can see a good chunk of Caspers Park from the West Ridge and visually follow your progress through Bell Canyon and beyond to the park entrance and San Juan Canyon. Facing east from the West Ridge Trail you can see the highest ridges and peaks of the Santa Ana Mountains including Saddleback and Mt. Piños.

To return to your car, descend Star Rise and make a quick left on the dirt road at the base of the ridge. You'll intersect Bell Canyon Road 0.2 miles later. Make a right turn and ride this trail the remaining distance to your car.

#5   Oso Trail

Mileage: 4.4 miles from Ortega Highway or 11.2 miles from Caspers Park
Water: Caspers Park only
Level of Difficulty: Intermediate
Elevation: Begin: 600+ feet. High point: 1,500+ feet. End: 600+ feet.

First, stop in at the Caspers Park kiosk to pay your park fees. Keep your paperwork with you and leave the orange ticket visible in your parked car out on the highway. You may have to show proof of payment if you are stopped by a Ranger.

Then, for the shorter variation of this ride, drive 3.4 miles on Highway 74 east of Caspers entry. On your left you will find a metal gate blocking the dirt road. Pass through the gate. Ride up the gently climbing Oso Trail road, parallel to a primitive and unnamed valley.

After 1 mile, the climb turns from gentle to steep. Within 1 more mile you gain more than 400 feet of elevation.

Atop this high ridge on Oso Trail, the views are wonderful. Rugged mountains and steep valleys surround you in a beautiful panorama of Southern California hill country. A left turn takes you shortly to the border of the park and the Audubon Preserve, where a road snakes along a ridge line to the west, returning to the main body of Caspers Park. However, *you may not cross the Audubon Society boundary nor may you drop from the ridge line into Starr Ranch.* Trespassing here means an individual might destroy valuable scientific research conducted by a prestigious environmental organization, and this has heavy moral overtones. No one wants to think of himself as an ecological "bad guy." We could decrease trespass problems, and I'd like to help Audubon if I could with this book. Reduced friction between Caspers and Audubon means a healthy mountain biking environment.

To return to your car, simply reverse your previous travel directions in a nice downhill run for a total of 4.4 miles.

If you want a longer ride, begin at the main entrance to Caspers Park and follow directions for Ride #3 for riding the Juaneño Trail. The valley of the Juaneño Trail consists of brushy grassland with trees standing tall along the creek beds. The ridges rise higher above the valley and become vertical palisades overlooking the basin of San Juan Creek. Follow this dirt road for over a mile, where it then becomes a firebreak that runs mainly along a fence line parallel to Ortega Highway. It then continues (3.4 miles total) across a creek bed to Oso Trail. On the way you pass Badger Pass Trail on your left.

The firebreak portion of the trip is on "disked" land. (A set of heavy metal disks towed by a tractor turns the soil over. They bury old growth and create a soft, bumpy surface.) As such, it requires a lot of energy to cross the uneven land. Needless to say, it isn't the favorite bike route in the park. Upon reaching the Oso Trail from this firebreak road, simply follow the route to the ridge as discussed in the first part of this ride description. Then, head back down Oso Trail to Highway 74, turn right on the Juaneño Trail and return to your vehicle.

#6   Hot Springs Canyon
Mileage: 3 miles round trip
Water: None
Level of Difficulty: Beginner
Elevation: Begin: 700+ feet. High point: 900+ feet. End: 700+ feet.
Campgrounds/Facilities: San Juan Hot Springs
Nearest Services: San Juan Capistrano

Getting There: Take I-5 to Highway 74 at San Juan Capistrano and drive east 12.5 miles (5 miles past the main entrance to Caspers Park). Turn left into a canyon with signs advertising San Juan Hot Springs. There are some Forest Service buildings on your left.

Park your car at the entrance to the canyon and ride your bike into the valley. The area is canopied by huge sycamore and oak trees. You ride along a pleasant road curving easily through the narrow ravine. After 1.5 miles the road is blocked by private property, signaling time for you to turn back.

The best part may have been saved for last, however: San Juan Hot Springs, a natural thermal spot, has been a resort in this area for over 100 years. You can pay to sit in a hot tub and you can picnic on the grounds here as well. It's a great way to end your ride.

CHAPTER 10

WHITING RANCH WILDERNESS PARK

Whiting Ranch is the newest of Orange County's public wilderness parks (1991). An interlocking series of oak-shaded valleys and high grassy ridges, the park seems much larger than its 1,500 acres. Whiting Park is also home to a group of rose-colored sandstone cliffs considered to be one of the county's most beautiful rock formations (Red Rock).

Whiting Ranch, part of an early land grant from the California governor to Jose Serrano in 1842, was originally called Rancho Cañada de Los Alisos. The Serranos farmed and raised cattle on their land until 1864, when a two-year drought that destroyed other local ranchos also finished off the Rancho Canada de Los Alisos. Banks foreclosed on loans as the creeks ran dry and the cattle died. (It was at this opportune moment that James Irvine bought his empire in Orange County for 50 cents an acre.) Farmed and developed over the past century, residential development began in earnest in 1959. Since then, suburban building has dominated the landscape, leaving Whiting Park as an oasis of natural land open to the public.

Just a few miles from Whiting Ranch Park on El Toro Road is McFadden Ranch Park. A collection of ranch buildings from the 1800s, McFadden Ranch is an interpretive center depicting farm life in agricultural Orange County as it was a hundred years ago. Though nearly in sight of Whiting Ranch, the current road system requires a round-about drive of several miles to reach McFadden Ranch Park. To get a view of the past, take El Toro Road east from I-5 and continue 7.5 miles. Find McFadden Ranch at the base of a tall hill on your left.

Whiting Ranch Wilderness Park
Water: Sculpture Garden area
Level of Difficulty: Beginner, intermediate
Elevation: 750+ feet to 1,600+ feet
Topo Maps: Orange County topo or USGS 7.5 minute series (El Toro)
Campground/Facilities: None
Parking: Enter from Portola Parkway and park in the paved lot or adjacent dirt lot

Getting There: Take the Lake Forest exit from I-5 in the El Toro area. Head east toward the hills. After 4.7 miles turn left on Portola Parkway. Continue 0.5 miles to the paved parking lot.

#1   Whiting Road Loop
Length: 5 miles round trip
Water: Sculpture Garden
Level of Difficulty: Intermediate
Elevation: Begin: 750+ feet. High point: 1,400+ feet. End: 700+ feet.

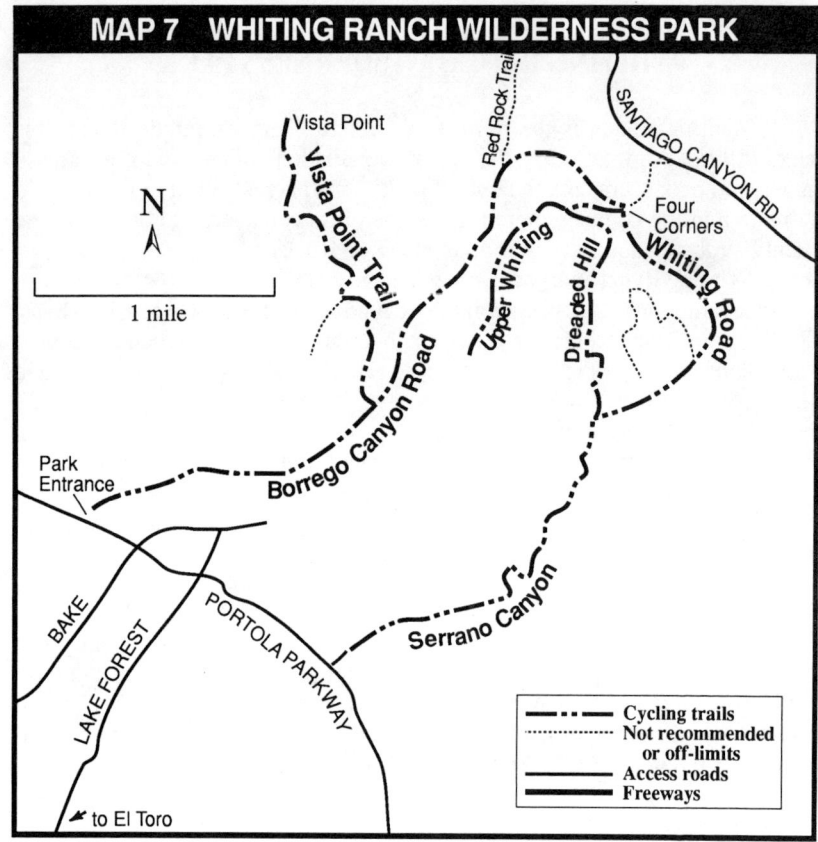

MAP 7 WHITING RANCH WILDERNESS PARK

N

1 mile

Vista Point

Vista Point Trail

Red Rock Trail

SANTIAGO CANYON RD.

Four Corners

Whiting Road

Upper Whiting

Dreaded Hill

Park Entrance

Borrego Canyon Road

Serrano Canyon

BAKE

LAKE FOREST

PORTOLA PARKWAY

to El Toro

——··— Cycling trails
············· Not recommended
   or off-limits
——— Access roads
▬▬▬ Freeways

From the parking lot go to the Sculpture Garden area at the park's entrance. See the trail dropping downhill and follow it into Borrego Valley. This small valley is very narrow but leads back into the larger body of the park.

The trail alternates between a dirt road and footpath. There are several creek crossings as you ride up the valley. The area is heavily wooded. In the spring the grass is lushly green, the whole area cool and shaded (not a bad thing, since you gain elevation through the whole canyon).

After about 3 miles, a hill looms before you at the end of a long dirt road. Reaching the top you'll find a crossroads called Four Corners, the convergence of four roads that provide access to the whole park. Make a left turn and ride a few yards. Another dirt road comes up from your right. Take this right and follow Whiting Road along the contour of the ridge to a distant electrical tower. The trail drops sharply down the end of the ridge line into a wooded valley (Serrano Canyon). From this spot you lose elevation ever so slowly. After approximately 2 miles you exit the valley near a wash and concrete bridge. As you come out onto Portola Parkway, make a right and begin the last mile back to the parking lot.

#2   Red Rock Trip
Length: 3.8 miles (includes short hike)
Water: Sculpture Garden
Level of Difficulty: Beginner
Elevation: Begin: 750+ feet. High point: 1,000+ feet. End: 750+ feet.

From the Sculpture Garden area ride down into Borrego Valley. Follow the trail, which quickly alternates from road to single-track trail through the sandy soil. You cross many creek beds (wet during a few months of the year) as the trail snakes its way through the narrow canyon.

After 1.4 miles you will find some park displays at the junction of two trails. The trail/road to the right leads to Four Corners. The foot trail beyond the displays leads into the Red Rock area. Park and lock your bikes and walk about 1/2 mile into Red Rock Canyon, where you see a rose-colored sandstone towering several hundred feet above you, eroded and strangely shaped.

Retrace your route to your car. For beginners, pedaling through these sandy conditions will probably make the distance of nearly 4 miles just about right.

If you want to continue into the rest of the park, simply take the main route east from the bicycle parking area. In another mile you'll reach Four Corners and connections to the rest of the park.

#3   Dreaded Hill Loop
Length: 4.5 miles
Water: Sculpture Garden
Level of Difficulty: Intermediate
Elevation: Begin: 750+ feet. High point: 1,624 feet. End: 700+ feet.

From the Sculpture Garden area of the park travel up Borrego Valley about 3 miles to Four Corners. On entering the intersection take a quick right and begin climbing the hill. This new trail is Whiting Road. Several hundred yards uphill another road intersects from the left. Turn left and continue a sharp climb up Dreaded Hill. At the top of this hill many smaller paths run here and there, leading to views of neighboring valleys and southern Orange County. Dreaded Hill Road crests at 1,624 feet, but this is just where the fun begins. The road takes a dive toward lower Serrano Canyon that doesn't stop for nearly 900 feet and 2 miles. It is steep and fast and heavily eroded. In addition, soil conditions are poor so that keeping control is a full-time job. The challenge is great and the ride good fun. Finally, you cross a dirt road near the bottom of Serrano Canyon. Take a right on Serrano Canyon Road and ride through a low-lying area of small trees and sandy soil. About 1.4 miles from the junction you exit the canyon. Note the wash and the concrete bridge to your left. Bear right onto Portola for the last mile to the parking lot. You've now entered the most dangerous part of your ride, a city street!

#4 Upper Whiting Road Trip

Length: 5.6 miles round trip
Water: Sculpture Garden area
Level of Difficulty: Intermediate
Elevation: Begin: 750+ feet. High point: 1,300+ feet. End: 750+ feet.

Enter the park from the Sculpture Garden area next to the paved parking lot. Weave your way through Borrego Valley past the turn-off for Red Rock and on to Four Corners. Make an immediate right, which puts you on Upper Whiting Road. Begin another steady climb around the contour of a ridge line. A short distance from Four Corners you'll see a road on the left, the beginning of Dreaded Hill. Pass by it, bearing to the right.

On Upper Whiting Road you are at the top of the high ridges. You can see back into the Santa Ana Mountains and the city of El Toro. Much of southern Orange County lies beneath you. This is a great spot to watch the flights of sleek fighter jets banking and turning around the El Toro Marine Airfield. Also, to the west, look down into the valley beneath you. You'll see a small ribbon of trail through the trees, the trail you came up through Borrego Canyon.

Upper Whiting Road ends at a fence atop the higher ridges just described. Do not proceed beyond the fence; the residential development area is closed to the public. One day you'll be able to cross over into the neighborhood and ride downhill to the park entrance. For now, however, you'll need to reverse your direction to return to the parking lot and your car.

#5 Vista Point Trail

Length: 4 miles
Water: Sculpture Garden area
Level of Difficulty: Intermediate
Elevation: Begin: 750+ feet. High point: 1,500+ feet. End: 750+ feet.

From the park's Sculpture Garden area ride up Borrego Valley 1 mile. You will come to a fence and directional signs. Turn left following the eroded dirt track up the hillside—Vista Point Trail. The first part of the climb is high and the road nastily eroded. Midway up the hillside the incline decreases. Riding gets easier until you pass through a saddle at the top of the ridge, then you ride a nearly flat trail around the contour of a hillside.

On this high ridge line you look out over Mission Viejo and south Orange County. The surrounding ridge and valleys provide delightful view. Spring rains turn the hills to a deep, rich green while flowers bloom radiantly.

Shortly after you enter the saddle area, you pass a road to the left. Do not enter—this is private land. Instead, follow the sign and keep right. At the bottom of a short, steep climb you can see Vista Hill off to the left. Climb to the top of the ridge and follow the road left to Vista Point. There you'll find shade and a flat spot for lunch or a rest stop. From the top you have a magnificent view. Across the park you can easily see the outstanding formations at Red Rock.

To return to your car simply retrace your route.

Photo: Mickey McTigue

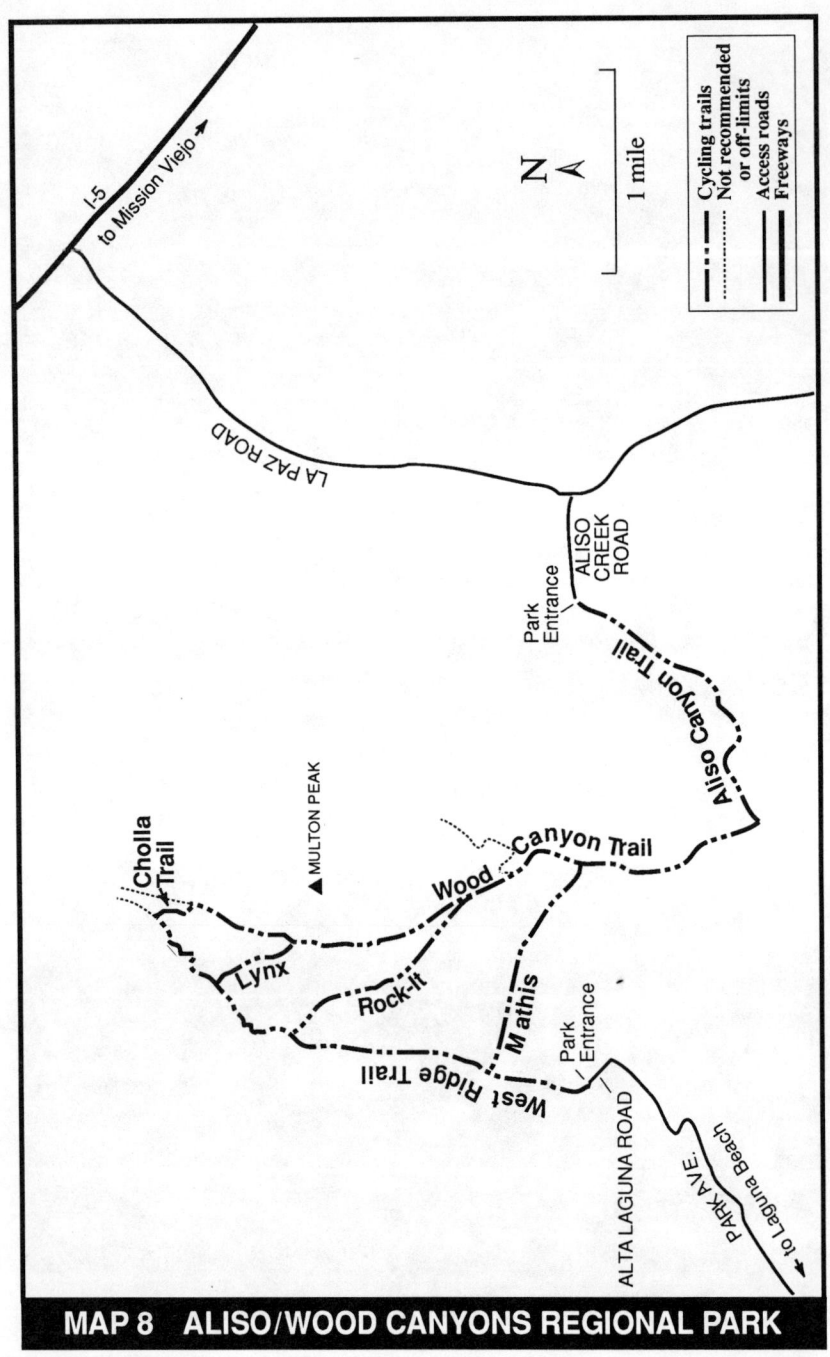

MAP 8 ALISO/WOOD CANYONS REGIONAL PARK

I-5
to Mission Viejo

LA PAZ ROAD

ALISO CREEK ROAD

Park Entrance

Aliso Canyon Trail

Cholla Trail

▲ MULTON PEAK

Wood Canyon Trail

Lynx

Rock-It

Mathis

West Ridge Trail

Park Entrance

ALTA LAGUNA ROAD

PARK AVE.

to Laguna Beach

N

1 mile

Cycling trails
Not recommended
or off-limits
Access roads
Freeways

CHAPTER 11

ALISO / WOOD CANYONS REGIONAL PARK

One of Orange County's best kept secrets is Aliso/Wood Canyons Regional Park. It lies hidden between Laguna Beach and Laguna Hills, a unique combination of city and county land. There are only two entrances to the park, and the park is not in the phone book.

The western portion of the park is part of the Laguna Beach Greenbelt. The high, lush ridges have been secured as a source of open space and recreation. A series of trails and roads criss-cross this area above Laguna Canyon Drive. From the ridge four other trails drop down into the park, which is county property. Together, these two parcels form an adult playground of over 5,000 acres.

In 1842 Juan Avila received this area as part of a 13,000-acre land grant (Rancho Niguel). The land has been used for farming and cattle grazing through the 1980s. Since then, suburban development has taken over the big California ranches.

Aliso/Wood Canyons Regional Park
Water: Laguna Beach entry, at Alta Laguna Park
Level of Difficulty: Intermediate, beginner
Elevation: Laguna Beach entry; high point: 1,036 feet
Topo Maps: USGS 7.5 minute series (Laguna Beach, San Juan Capistrano)

Getting There: From I-5 in Laguna Hills take La Paz Road south to Aliso Creek Road. Turn right and go 0.5 miles to the park entry signs. You will cross Aliso Creek and bear to your left to enter the dirt parking lot area.

From Pacific Coast Highway in downtown Laguna Beach, turn onto Laguna Avenue (across from the old Laguna Hotel, one of the city's most famous landmarks). Head inland, and after one block, Laguna Avenue becomes Park Avenue. Park Avenue leads through the city, high into the hills directly to Alta Laguna Boulevard. Turn left and go 200 yards. On your right is a park. The ridge bike path begins at the street's dead-end. The highest point in Laguna Beach lies within the park: the locals call it "Top of the World," and the view is fabulous.

#1 Top of the World Run
Length: 5 miles
Water: In city park off Alta Laguna
Level of Difficulty: Intermediate, beginner (slow descent)
Elevation: Begin: 1,036 feet. Low point: 600+ feet. End: 1,036 feet.

Enter the Greenbelt trails from the dead-end of Alta Laguna. Follow the main dirt road—West Ridge Trail—as it quickly drops down the spine of the high ridge line. This is mountain biker freefall, until you find large patches of grooved rock rushing toward you in the road. (You find that sort of thing a lot in the Aliso/Wood area. Exercise caution!)

The path is alternately easy and technical down the ridge. At 0.6 miles the Mathis Road turnoff appears on your right; pass it and continue along the main road. At 1.6 miles note a water tower and facilities on your left. Below them, to the right another major trail drops down into the valley (Rock-It Trail). Ignore this trail and continue down the ridge. At 2.3 miles you pass the Lynx Trail on your right. Very steep and poorly maintained, this trail is more suited to hiking than biking.

Finally, a short distance beyond Lynx you'll see a foot trail on the right. This is the Cholla Trail, the last major track down to Wood Canyon. This single track trail is well maintained and the downhill run excellent. (A little beyond Cholla Trail the road ends abruptly at a gate.)

To return simply retrace your steps, but it's uphill this time! There's over 400 feet of elevation gain to get back to your car.

From the Laguna Beach side of Aliso/Wood Canyons, this West Ridge Trail is the key to the rest of the park. From here you can reach Mathis and Wood canyons or continue down to the Laguna Hills entrance. The downhills off this ridge are great!

#2   Mathis/Cholla Loop
Length: 6.7 miles
Water: City Park
Level of Difficulty: Intermediate (Caution advised!)

From the end of Alta Laguna begin the long downhill run atop the ridge line. At 0.6 miles make a right turn on an old dirt road, the Mathis Trail. In the space of half a mile you drop an unbelievable 500 feet so fast you don't know if you're having fun or being terrorized. The trail is a roller coaster ride on dirt followed by rocks scattered over cracked and fallen slabs of grooved stone. The trail surface alternates back and forth until the final descent—a long, well graded dirt road to the bottom of Mathis Canyon.

Mathis Canyon is a flat grassy area with picturesque stands of oak and sycamore scattered about. To your left is a high ridge, and the road you're on parallels that ridge as you ride. After a short distance you come to a trail junction. Turn left. You go around the ridge line and enter Wood Canyon on the other side.

Wood Canyon, full of trees and with a small seasonal stream running through it, is lush and green in the springtime. The canyon begins a gradual ascent that doesn't end until you intersect with Cholla Trail 2.5 miles up the road. Turn left on Cholla Trail, working your way to the top of the Laguna Ridge. When you crest the ridge, turn left, beginning your 2.5 mile return to Alta Laguna and your car.

The summer heat can make Orange County bike riding uncomfortable or even undesirable. These canyons, though, offer year-round riding, since the park's proximity to the ocean keeps temperatures down. After some experimentation you'll find the best times to ride in the hot months, June to October.

#3   Rock-It/Cholla Loop
Length: 7.1 miles
Water: City Park off Alta Laguna
Level of Difficulty: Intermediate
Elevation: Begin: 1,036 feet. Low point: 200+ feet. End: 1,036 feet.

From the dead-end of Alta Laguna, being your long descent atop the West Ridge Trail. At 1.6 miles you'll see a water tank and facilities to your left. Turn right on a road that intersects nearby. You're now on the Rock-It Trail.

I'm not sure how the trail received its name. But there's a lot of rock everywhere, and the trail has all the excitement of Rock n' Roll as the steep terrain makes for rocket-like acceleration—more than you'll need or want.

This downhill is a thoroughly challenging trail: steep drops, rocky paths and eroded soil. As the trail approaches the lower end of the ridge you see a path to the left and another to the right. This is the beginning of a large meadow. Take the left path; the right is for hikers only.

Cross through the grassy meadow, which has immense old trees. After about 1/4 mile you enter a steep creek embankment. On the other side turn left onto Wood Canyon Trail, the dirt road that runs prominently through the valley.

Continue through the valley another several miles until you see Cholla Trail on your left. It is marked by brown park signs, but there is no mention of the name Cholla. (County Rangers report that new trail signs are on their way.)

After you reach the Laguna Ridge again, turn left from Cholla Trail onto the main trail to return to your car. It's uphill all the way (about 400 feet)—time to pay for all the fun you had!

#4   Old Corral Trip
Length: 5 miles
Water: None
Level of Difficulty: Beginner
Elevation: Begin: 100 feet. High point: 200+ feet. End: 100 feet.

This trail is absolutely perfect for the first time rider. Table flat and pretty well free of debris, the area is a large, grassy plain divided by hills and ridges. Many of the hilly areas have small caves and interesting rock formations.

Begin at the Laguna Hills entry off Aliso Creek Road. As you leave the parking area, follow the signs and take the alternate trail parallel to Awma Road (this road is closed to bike use) approximately 1.5 miles to the gate at the beginning of Wood Canyon Trail. Take the Wood Canyon Trail 1 mile through a series of pastures, valleys and hills. Your destination is an old abandoned horse corral, a great place for a rest stop. From the corral you turn around and retrace your path back down Wood Canyon Road and back to the parking lot.

This is a very easy-going route for any first-time mountain biker you're introducing to the sport. With enticing scenery the physical demands upon your guests are not so onerous as to discourage them from future riding.

#5   Aliso/Wood Canyons Loop
Length: 10.2 miles
Water: None
Level of Difficulty: Intermediate
Elevation: Begin: 100+ feet. High point: 850+ feet. End: 100+ feet.

Begin at the Laguna Hills entry off Aliso Creek Road. Take the trail alongside Awma Road from the parking lot 1.5 miles to the gate at Wood Canyon Road. Go through the gate and up Wood Canyon Road through the lush grasslands. Continue past the entry to Mathis Canyon (on your left) and, after 1 mile, ride into the main area of Wood Canyon. Keep left on the main trail. If the day is warm, this canyon will provide welcome relief. The many trees here shade you as you slowly gain more than 300 feet in elevation up to the turnoff on Cholla Trail).

At Cholla Trail the work begins in earnest. Make a left turn on the well signed path and quickly gain 100 feet. When you reach the top of the Laguna ridge line, turn left beginning a 2-mile ride and a 200-foot gain uphill toward the Mathis Trail. After a good, steady climb take the Mathis Trail on your left. Begin the descent, then the free-fall into Mathis Canyon. In what seems like seconds from the ridge line you find yourself on the last stretch of dirt road plummeting toward Mathis Canyon below.

At the bottom of the hill continue straight ahead along Mathis Canyon Trail until you intersect with Wood Canyon. Turn right and follow the road to the metal gate. Turn left beyond the gate, riding the last 1.5 miles to your car.

Variations: It's possible to reverse directions on the park loop trail. You can do this by climbing the Mathis or Rock-It trails. Mathis is the steepest and most difficult of the two. Rock-It Trail is the easiest climb, though hardly a breeze as hill climbs go. These variations allow you to crest the Laguna Beach ridge line, ride downhill, and descend Cholla Trail, a very enjoyable single track.

CHAPTER 12

CRYSTAL COVE STATE PARK: MORO CANYON

The very last stretch of open coastal land in Orange County's San Joaquin Hills is a part of Crystal Cove State Park. The area consists of a series of lush valleys and rolling hills high above the Pacific between Laguna Beach and Corona Del Mar. Year after year, the surrounding open areas are transformed piecemeal into suburbia. However, Crystal Cove State Park has saved several priceless coastal areas for public use. Among them is a 3,000-acre paradise called Moro Canyon. In the stillness of the coastal canyons and the shade of the tall trees you can imagine what this land was like not so long ago.

The canyon areas of the park comprises four main ridges and two valleys, running primarily north and south. Abundant plant life and seasonal streams combine to make a lovely place with just about every kind of mountain biking terrain imaginable. The major valley, Moro Canyon, is the main route north and south through the preserve. From Moro Canyon you can intersect with the many connecting trails, going anywhere into the park backcountry.

The early Spanish map makers called this place "Lomarias de la Costa" (ridge of hills on the coast). This area was a part of Rancho San Joaquin, one of the many land grant cattle ranches that dominated early California. Jose de Sepulveda, the original grantee, received about 20,000 acres from the California governor in 1836. The land was sold to James Irvine in the 1860s: he purchased nearly half of modern-day Orange County for about 50 cents an acre.

The lands around Moro Canyon have been used for farming and grazing from the early Spanish/Mexican days until late into the 20th century. The forested valley and chaparral-covered hills offer beauty and challenge to the mountain cyclist.

Crystal Cove State Park
Facilities: Large parking lot, restrooms, and a nature center. Rangers' headquarters and is your only source of water.
Topo Maps: USGS 7.5 minute series (Laguna Beach)

Getting There: From the 405 Freeway, take Laguna Canyon Road exit into Laguna Beach. Laguna Canyon dead-ends into Pacific Coast Highway. Turn right, heading north on Pacific Coast Highway 2 miles or so to the El Morro Canyon sign. Turn right. (There's a school on the corner.) Head up the small road and into the park. Park your car here and pay the State Park fee of $5 (there's a vending machine just outside the Ranger Headquarters.)

You can create many combinations of trails in Moro Canyon. Though small, this area combines both physical and technical challenge with great natural beauty. It also packs in a lot of fun and is probably the most popular mountain bike riding site in Orange County.

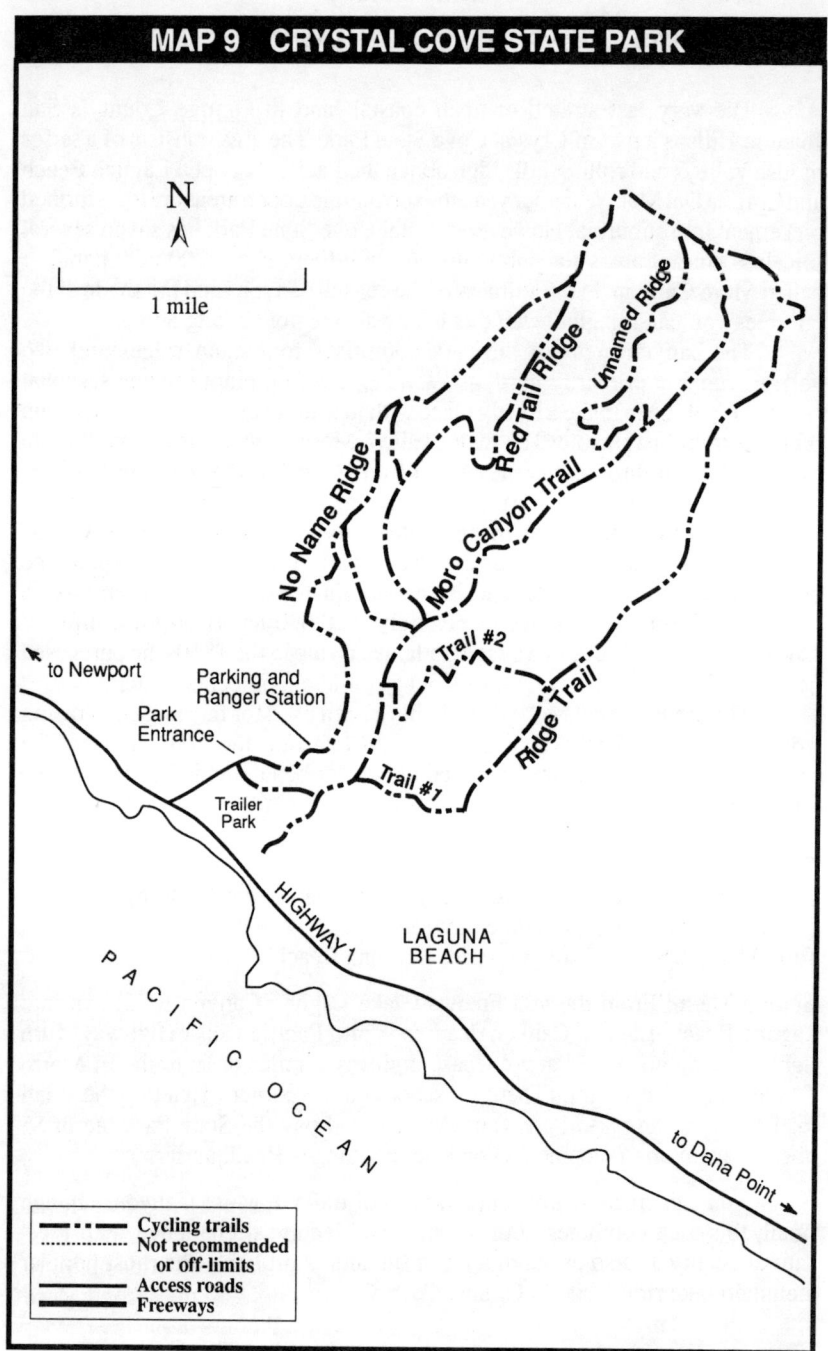

MAP 9   CRYSTAL COVE STATE PARK

N

1 mile

No Name Ridge

RedTail Ridge

Unnamed Ridge

Moro Canyon Trail

Trail #2

Ridge Trail

to Newport

Parking and
Ranger Station

Park
Entrance

Trail #1

Trailer
Park

HIGHWAY 1

LAGUNA
BEACH

PACIFIC OCEAN

to Dana Point

Cycling trails
Not recommended
or off-limits
Access roads
Freeways

#1 Moro Canyon

Mileage: 5.5 miles
Water: Parking lot
Level of Difficulty: Beginner
Elevation Gain: 400+ feet
Campground/Facilities: None in valley
Nearest Services: Corona Del Mar/Laguna Beach

Ride south from the parking lot toward the park entrance. Turn left on the dirt road that parallels the trailer park. The road drops 60 feet over the space of a couple hundred yards. Extreme beginners may wish to dismount and walk their bikes to flatter terrain below.

Moro Canyon begins at the bottom of the hill. Slowly and steadily the well graded trail rises through a lovely valley of golden pasturelands dotted with trees and brush. Beginners can look forward to a moderate workout in an atmosphere of rural beauty.

Two miles up the canyon find a grove of huge, gnarled oak trees. Take a moment to rest there in the cool shade. Admire the ancient trees flanked by a rock wall carved over time into grottoes and small caves.

Continue up the canyon a short distance through oak forest and pass into an open area. You'll see on the left a road climbing up a hillside to the top of Red Tail Ridge, referred to as West Loop. Your ascent ends here.

Turn around for the gentle descent taking you back to the mobile home park at the bottom of Moro Canyon. Continue following the road uphill to the parking area.

#2 Moro Ridge Route

Mileage: 6 miles
Water: None, last water at parking lot
Level of Difficulty: Moderate, steep
Elevation Gain: 900+ feet
Water: Parking lot
Campground: Campground in park
Nearest Services: Corona Del Mar / Laguna Beach

Ride to Moro Canyon Trail as described in Ride #1. Just a hundred yards or so past the trailer park is the first connector trail heading right to Moro Ridge. Previously closed to the public, Trail #1 was re-opened in September 1992. Once on Moro Ridge, point your bike up (northward), then walk n' ride a gnarly 1/3 mile or so. Farther up the ridge, the elevation becomes more gradual and you begin a long ascent. You travel from the 300 foot range to over 1,000 feet elevation at the far north end of the park. It is a good workout with great views. The trip down is fast and fun, and the track is solid and relatively clean of debris.

You can also reach Moro Ridge on a more gradual route. Ride up Moro Canyon about 1 mile from the trailer park and turn right on the second Moro Ridge connector trail. This gradual trail follows the contours of the land and is "do-able," but strenuous. Caution: The trail could make you hot and sweaty, or cause you to breathe hard, but the ride down is electrifying.

Atop the ridge, looking to the north end of Moro Canyon, you find one of the park's more distinctive features: a stretch of narrow trail, "single track" for those who enjoy this type of ride.

Approximately 200 to 300 yards before reaching the northern end of Moro Ridge Trail, leave the main road through an entry in a wire fence onto a foot trail. Follow that trail to the top of the hill (elevation 1,000+ feet) and down the other side to a fence line. The trail then continues for about a mile, twisting and turning, climbing and diving along the northern park boundary fence.

This single track lies on the high main ridge of the San Joaquin Hills. Among the coastal scrub and cactus there are views west and east along the ridge and down into Moro Canyon.

The challenge of this ride is undeniable as the view switches from panoramic to the immediate area around the front wheel of your bike. Sharp turns, steep drops, roots, rocks, spiny cactus, and unstable soil combine to demand all your attention and skill. This is first and foremost a technical ride.

Occasionally, you may lose the trail into a small chunk of dirt road. Always bear to the right. Go for the fence line until the end. This 1-mile trail takes you across three of the four major ridgelines and their interconnecting trails.

On these hillsides there used to be a little cactus that grazing cattle ate for brunch, keeping it in check. Now, however, it's spread everywhere and often grows quite close to the trail. Since this is a State Park, all plant species are protected. I urge you to ride cautiously, lest you knock down these cactus plants, damaging their tender spines and ravaging their flesh with your big strong bodies.

About 1/2 mile after entering the single track trail, the path dumps out onto the Moro Canyon Trail. To return to the parking lot you have two options:

(1) A left turn takes you down a steep, hard, eroded surface (like riding down a washboard with ball bearings on it). Extreme caution is advised. This trail eventually takes you back to your car.

(2) A right turn from where the single track enters the same road will take you uphill a hundred yards or so to a junction of three trails (a much less treacherous route). Turn left and a dirt road gently descends 0.5 miles or so along an unnamed ridge line. At the southern tip of this ridge, the road drops abruptly, beginning a steep descent to Moro Canyon Trail on the valley floor. This is the route that returns you to the parking lot. The Canyon Road drops ever so gently through lovely shaded oak groves and grasslands. This portion of the ride is visually pleasant and blessedly downhill!

#3 Red Tail Ridge Route via "No Name" Ridge

Mileage: 6 miles
Water: Parking lot
Level of Difficulty: Moderate, steep
Elevation Gain: 1,000+ feet
Campgrounds: Campground in park
Nearest Services: Corona Del Mar / Laguna Beach

At the north end of the parking lot, a trail forks. Bear right for a long and steady ascent up the contours of "No Name" Ridge. It's a great climb with solid elevation gains, and it's a great workout if you like to breathe hard. When you intersect the other road atop the ridge, you've gained nearly 400 feet!

Topping "No Name" Ridge, you find one of the park's best views. From this grassy knoll look northwest to see a beautiful section of coastline stretching into the distance. Gaze inland to see many of the highest peaks and ridges of the San Joaquin Hills. To the east you peer into Moro Canyon hundreds of feet below.

Continue following the ridge trail north. A trail appears to the right and dives steeply towards the valley below. (It plummets from about 600 feet to 100 feet at the bottom of Moro Canyon in the space of 3/4 mile. Wild, it screams into the void like a falling smart bomb. This is a marvelous run!)

Continuing along "No Name" Ridge, the trail climbs to a small hill and then levels off a bit. (The trail becomes a fenced off dead-end about 100 yards ahead.) Go downhill to your right on a single track trail. This trail descends the side of the ridge sharply at first, then more gently until you arrive at the bottom of a canyon (below "No Name" Ridge on one side and Red Tail Ridge on the other). Here you'll find the traditional California oak and sycamore valley dominated by seasonal creeks. There is also a campground, a pleasant place to take a break. The trail becomes a dirt road heading north. It soon begins to climb steeply and is badly eroded all the way up. (The reverse downhill run requires some careful attention on your part.) This trail climbs finally to the top of Red Tail Ridge, intersecting the main north-south ridge trail.

To Return to the Parking Lot: By turning north (left), you return to the fence line single-track. A turn south (right) takes you down the length of Red Tail Ridge. This is another breath-taking drop that goes from 570 feet to under 100 feet elevation as you twist and turn along the ridge contours. For the first half mile or so the ridge drops steeply. The rock slab trail falls like a stairway, six inches to a foot each step down the hill with ruts and rocks everywhere. Cactus silently reach out to greet you. When you finish you feel like you've been riding a jackhammer!

This incredible power dive finally empties out onto Moro Canyon Trail, and a right turn points you toward the parking lot.

MAP 10 SANTIAGO OAKS REGIONAL PARK / ANAHEIM HILLS

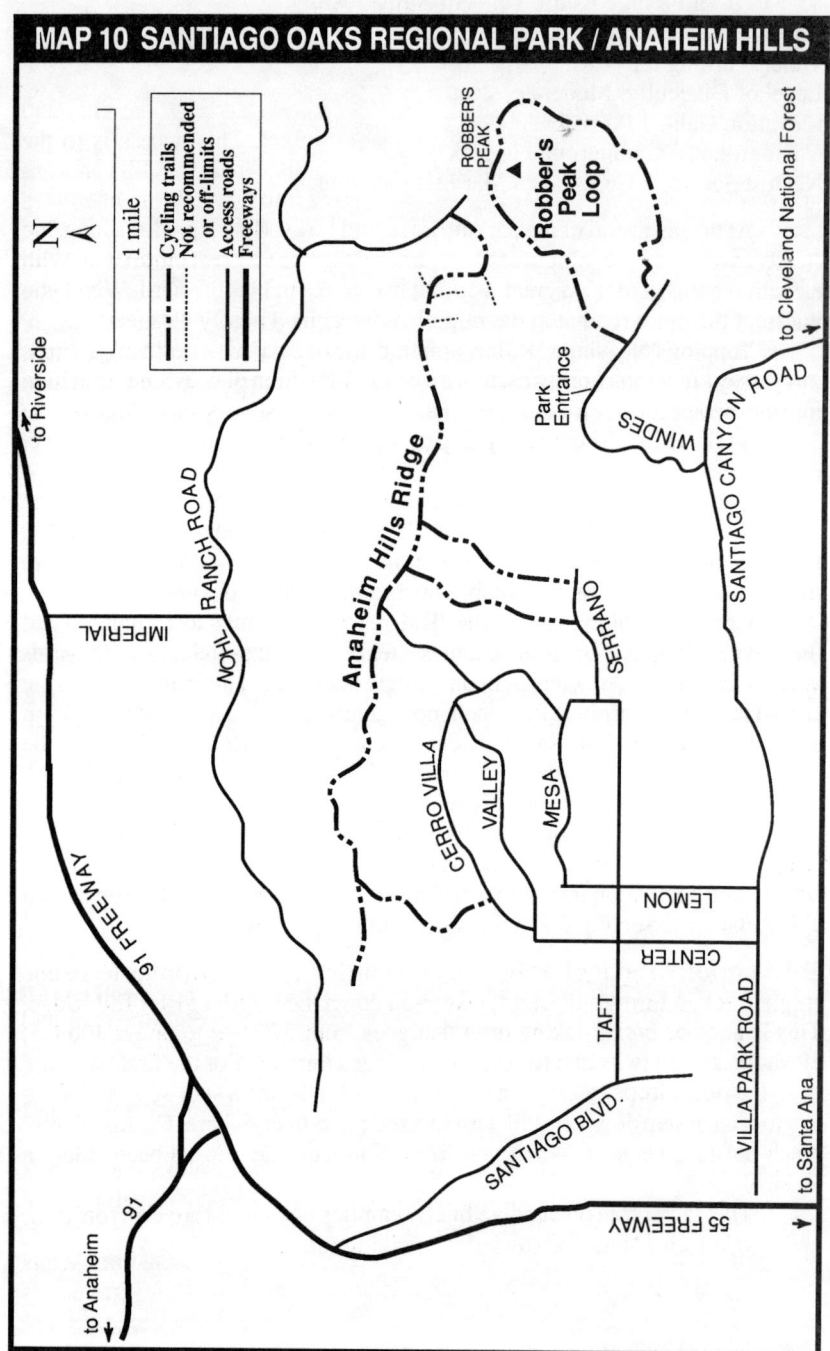

Cycling trails
Not recommended
or off-limits
Access roads
Freeways

N

1 mile

Robber's Peak Loop

ROBBER'S PEAK

to Cleveland National Forest

SANTIAGO CANYON ROAD

WINDES

Park Entrance

to Riverside

NOHL RANCH ROAD

IMPERIAL

Anaheim Hills Ridge

SERRANO

CERRO VILLA

VALLEY

MESA

LEMON

CENTER

91 FREEWAY

TAFT

VILLA PARK ROAD

SANTIAGO BLVD.

to Anaheim

91

55 FREEWAY

to Santa Ana

CHAPTER 13

SANTIAGO REGIONAL PARK / ANAHEIM HILLS

Santiago Oaks Regional Park, small by county standards, has only 250 acres, but it does offer access to the mountain biker. This access is to the Anaheim Hills Trail System. The higher ridges in the Anaheim Hills area are open to both horses and bikes, with several miles of trails available to interested mountain bikers.

On clear days views from the tops of the high ridges are impressive. With rural Orange County as a backdrop, Catalina is often visible. You can see all the way across north Orange County and well into Los Angeles County.

Although the Santiago Oaks Park/Anaheim Hills is not true backcountry, its greatest virtue is accessibility to north Orange County. It is a nice place to ride—a good place to jump on your bike and do what you like to do!

#1 Santiago Oaks Regional Park / Robber's Peak Loop
Mileage: 2.5 miles
Water: Santiago Oaks Regional Park
Level of Difficulty: Intermediate (O.K. for practiced beginners)
Elevation: Begin: 460+ feet. High point: 1,152+ feet. End: 460+ feet.
Topo Maps: Orange County topo or USGS 7.5 minute series (Orange)
Campgrounds: None
Nearest Services: City of Orange

Getting There: From the 55 Freeway near the City of Orange, take Katella east. The distance to the park is 3.9 miles, but the succession of streets can be confusing. Katella becomes Villa Park Drive within 0.5 miles of the freeway (same street). Villa Park Drive changes to Santiago Canyon Road. At mile 3 from the freeway turn left at Windes Drive and continue a short distance to the park, which is signed.

Bring two crisp "Yankee Dollar" bills to feed to the parking machine at the regional park. It is illegal to park your car near the gated park entrance.

From the front parking lot follow a path through a stone wall and down into a ravine (Santiago Creek). A small trail takes you up the opposite bank and onto a dirt road. Turn right on the road, which is quite flat for several hundred yards. Finally it cuts left into the Anaheim Hills and begins climbing sharply (approximately 700 feet in 1.2 miles) to your goal—Robber's Peak, the highest point on the tallest ridge of the Anaheim Hills.

From Robber's Peak ride east to the next ridge line. Follow the trail that circles around the power line tower and down the top of a high ridgeline. Take this southwesterly road back to Santiago Oaks Regional Park.

The road eventually shrinks to a trail near the end of the ridgeline. At this point, the trail drops most steeply to the valley floor below. At several points you'll want to walk your bike over bad trail sections instead of killing yourself.

At the bottom of the ridge turn right on one of the many roads leading back toward Santiago Regional Park.

#2 Anaheim Hills Ridge Loop

Mileage: Depends on route
Water: None
Level of Difficulty: Intermediate
Elevation: Begin: 600+ feet. High point: 1,000+ feet. End: 600+ feet
Topo Maps: Orange County topo or USGS 7.5 minute series (Orange)
Campgrounds: None
Nearest Services: Anaheim Hills, 2 miles west

Getting There: Take the 55 Freeway to the 91 Freeway east. Exit Imperial Highway, turn right and drive south to Nohl Ranch Road. Turn right on Nohl Ranch Road, drive to the corner of Serrano and Nohl Ranch Road and park.

Turn right at the school on the corner of Serrano and Nohl Ranch Road. Follow the trail leading past a dead-end barrier down into a gully. Take the path up into the hills. Once atop the ridge you have several riding options:

A) Continue along the ridge to its end, then return to your car. B) Drop down one of the four main trails leading off the high ridge, then loop back up to the ridge via another one of these trails. C) Drop down off the main ridge via one of the four roads, then follow the street map to Santiago Oaks Regional Park. From here take the main trail back into the Anaheim Hills above the school and drop down to your parked car.

You may also drive to the base of the four main trails that intersect the ridge trail, and ride up to the ridge. These are described below from west to east.

1) Cerro Villa Drive, between Rita and Loma. Go to the end of the cul-de-sac. Against the hills to the right, you'll see a trail going up the ridge. It makes an abrupt right turn going up a canyon and then heads steadily to the top of the high ridge road.

2) Cerro Villa snakes through the hills, becoming Mesa Drive at the corner of Valley Drive. Here there is an open gate with a trail leading off into the hills. As it ascends sharply, go left on this trail, climbing parallel to the border of the Edison Power Facility. The trail climbs directly to the high ridgeline and main trail. There are numerous side trails throughout this area surrounding the Edison Facility, and it's a great place to explore.

3) A major entryway is located at the corner of Serrano and Yellowstone. The trail follows up the right side of a small ravine heading way back into the hills. From a dead-end, the trail heads uphill, turning sharply right onto a small ridge. To continue to the high ridge, bear left and uphill. (This trail is just east of the Edison power station.)

4) The fourth entryway starts at the dead-end of Serrano, descends into a ravine and goes steeply uphill on a good path. At the top of the first ridge, it begins leveling off a little as it continues to the high ridge.

CHAPTER 14

CHINO HILLS STATE PARK: EAST ENTRY

Who'd have believed it? Twelve thousand acres of prime ranch country open to you and me in Orange County! One small corner of peace remaining in a too-fast world.

Chino Hills is like all the other gorgeous oak-dotted hill country you've ever seen in California, the kind of place that makes you want to jump on your bike and ride off into the sunset. This is the type of country you might have seen in old "Zorro" black and whites but didn't, due to budgetary constraints.

Chino Hills is a land of seasons, fields of gold and brown most of the year. It's a world gone green in winter and spring, the optimum seasons for riding in the park when temperatures are moderate and air quality usually good. In summer and fall—when daytime temperatures are extremely high and when smog can obscure the views or be physically harmful—it's best to ride in early morning or evening.

Air quality permitting, views across north and south ridges are spectacular when snow covers the local mountains. Chino Hills Park is a great place to ride and unwind; it's close to the city and easy to get to. For riding, views, and open space, Chino Hills State Park is a key community resource.

Getting There: From north Orange County take the 55 Freeway to the 91 Freeway and head east toward Corona.

At Prado Dam take the off-ramp for Highway 71 north (toward Pomona). Continue north on this busy, narrow road 6 miles to Pomona-Rincon Road. Turn left and continue along Pomona-Rincon a short distance north past a brick works to Soquel Canyon Drive. Turn left and drive another mile to Elinvar Drive. Turn left again. After a very short distance on Elinvar turn right onto a dirt road and begin driving up into the hills. In a mile you'll reach the boundary of the park. Continue through a gate and down a gently descending road through Bane Valley.

At the end of Bane Valley you pass the campground up around a hill. In another 1/4 mile you'll find the Ranger Headquarters with public parking.

The headquarters, a treat to see, is the old Rolling M Ranch, whose buildings have been converted for use as public facilities. The former ranch house is the park office, and the former barn is used as a work area. The windmill water pumps still stand as reminders of the area's ranching history.

Water Supplies: the campground at the south end of Bane Valley has several water spigots by the side of the road. These are the only sources of drinking water in the park. The water available to you from these pipes is for emergency use only; although safe, because of its taste no one would *willingly* drink it! It's best to bring your own water—a minimum of two quarts per person.

Topo Maps: Orange County topo or USGS 7.5 minute series (Prado Dam)

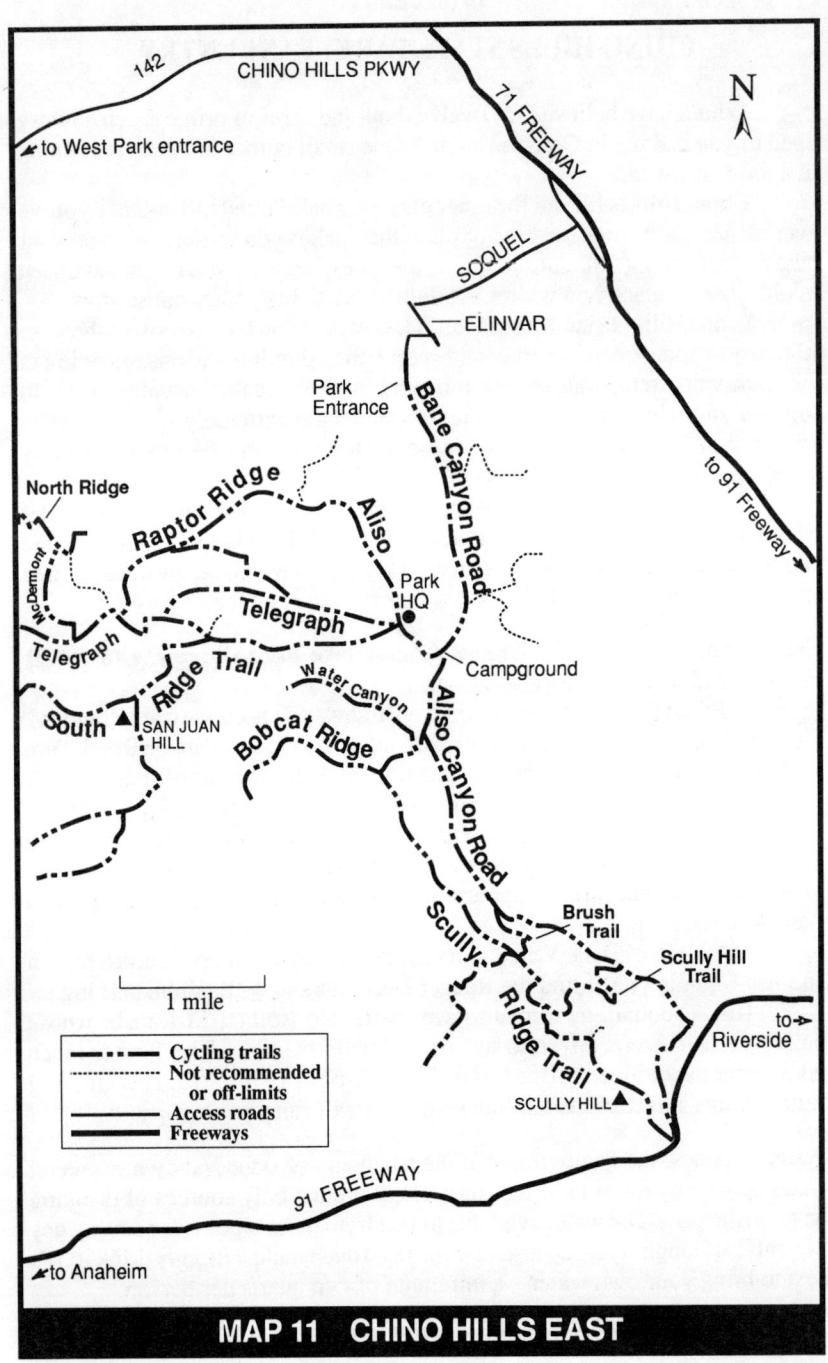

MAP 11 CHINO HILLS EAST

#1 Ranch through Aliso Valley and Return

Length: 8 miles
Water: Camping area
Level of Difficulty: Beginner
Elevation: Begin: 700+ feet. End of canyon: 400+ feet. End: 700+ feet.

From Park Headquarters, take your bike south on the blacktop road. Just after leaving the ranch area you pass a dirt road on your right, the trailhead for the Telegraph Canyon Trail. In another 100 yards you'll pass a second dirt road on the right. This is the beginning of South Ridge Trail, the park's longest trail.

Keep following the blacktop street around a hill and down toward the campground. Turn right into the camping area and ride the dirt road to a metal gate. Take your bike through the special opening in the gate and begin your ride.

Entering Aliso Canyon (south) is a visual experience. Vast expanses of the valley bottom are filled with lush fields of wild oats and large oak trees, gnarled and very old. The entire scene is strikingly beautiful, open and wide.

The main Aliso Valley Trail (north and south) is intersected by trails at many points. Some are okay to use and others are not. Trails from the east side of the valley all dead-end into private land. Do not ride these trails. Trails from the west side of the canyon are okay to use.

Half a mile from the camp area find your first connector trail, which leads to Water Canyon, Scully Ridge Trail and Bobcat Ridge Trail (see Ride #4). Pass by this first set of trails, and continue south into Aliso Canyon. As you ride you'll notice small roads dead-ending into gullies and at the base of hills. Often there are manhole covers at the end of the roads, water wells tended by the local water district. Beneath Chino Hills State Park is a rich aquifer whose waters supply Orange County.

Riding down the valley 1.8 miles from the campground entry you'll pass a second connector trail on the right. This is Brush Canyon Trail, one large switchback climbing to the top of the western ridge (over 400 feet of elevation gain). [This is a climb I recommend to all muscle freaks and other like-minded mortifiers of the flesh. As you'd expect from such a steep trail the downhill run is hot, the kind that broken bones are made of. *Caution advised.* (15 mph limit).]

Riding farther south through Aliso Canyon, at 2.6 miles from the campground you pass Scully Hill Trail on your right. It rises abruptly to the Scully Trail with over 500 feet of elevation gain. Yes, it's a challenging ride both up and down the Western Ridge.

Moving south from this last connector trail you come to the end of Aliso Valley at a well-marked metal gate. To return to the ranch area, retrace your steps up the valley. The elevation gain on your 4 mile return is 300 feet, so gradual as to be nearly unnoticeable. In terms of work and visual beauty, this is an ideal beginners' mountain bike ride.

Aliso Valley to Scully Trail: It's possible to link up with the Scully Trail from Aliso Valley beyond the park's southern boundary. Pass through the park entry gate down a dirt road for about a hundred yards until you come to a second dirt road. Turn right and ride a short distance to a stock gate. The gate opens out onto a large meadow. (Cyclists have permission to cross this land. Since horses are sometimes grazed here, you must re-lock each opened gate to prevent lost animals.) In less than half a mile the road passes south through the large meadow. The dirt road winds around the end of the West Ridge a short distance from some railroad tracks. On the right you'll find a blacktop road descending from the West Ridge above. Ride up the blacktop, which gives way to dirt higher up—the south end of the Scully Ridge Trail.

Horses: I know nothing about horses; they intimidate me. But one day as I was riding with a friend, I passed a large group of horses in this meadow. My buddy showed me how to stop, then walk forward slowly so as not to frighten the animals. He put out his hands to reassure them and within a few moments several horses became downright friendly! We then rode slowly away without spooking any of the animals. This seemed like a good way to handle the problem. When you're in doubt, always ask the horseback rider.

#2 Ranch to Bane Canyon Park Entrance and Return
Length: 4.4 miles
Level of Difficulty: Beginner
Elevation: Begin: 700+ feet. High point: 1,000+ feet. End: 700 feet

Turn south from the ranch parking area. Follow the blacktop road past the camping area and water spigots. The road curves north, turns to dirt and begins a long, slow climb uphill.

This is a good workout for the beginning mountain biker. The climb from the camping area to the peak gate is 2 miles with a 300 feet elevation gain. The ride back downhill is fast enough to thrill newcomers without killing them (although caution is always advised).

Bane Canyon Road sits in a narrow valley surrounded by steep rolling hills. The canyon is dominated by tall sycamore trees, green in spring and summer and golden in fall and winter. The park entrance at the gate on top of the hill is a good spot to rest before returning to the ranch and your car. The return trip is mostly a long glide down Bane Canyon. At the camping area you have a small uphill, but thereafter the road is easy with the ranch just ahead.

#3 South Ridge Trail Loop
Length: 4 miles
Level of Difficulty: Intermediate
Elevation: Begin: 700+ feet. High point: 1,300+ feet. End: 700+ feet.

Point your bike south from the ranch parking area. The first trail you see on your right is Telegraph Canyon Trail. Continue a few more yards and you'll see the beginning of the South Ridge Trail behind a gate to your right.

Turn right onto a dirt road and begin a long, steady climb atop the high ridge. There are no trees on this part of South Ridge. The unobstructed views get better the higher you climb. You can see Aliso Valley north to south as you ride; to the west is San Juan Hill and below that the Main Divide area. The mountain borders of the park surround you. To the north lie the San Gabriel Mountains, which you can spot even through the smog.

The grade up the South Ridge is steady and maintainable. Coming back down the other side is quick indeed. The road surface is a good quality black clay in most places except for a few eroded chasms large enough to swallow a Buick (a little rain can do horrors for these roads).

When you come to the three-way trail junction 1.2 miles from the beginning of South Ridge Trail, take the trail that angles downhill to the right, heading toward the Main Divide. (The left-hand trail heads farther up the ridge. The extreme right-hand road is a dead-end.)

Follow the trail 0.4 miles to a "Y" junction and turn right onto Telegraph Canyon East. (The left road goes down to Telegraph Canyon West). The first portion of this trail is very steep. Later, the road drops less radically but still the trail is fast, and before you know it, you're exiting the trail at the blacktop road. Turn left to the parking area and your car.

#4   Bobcat Ridge from Ranch Area
Length: 6 miles
Level of Difficulty: Intermediate
Elevation: Begin: 700+ feet. High point: 1,400+ feet. End: 700+ feet

Leave the ranch parking lot heading south. Follow the blacktop road to the campground. Turn right. Continue on the dirt road to the metal gate. Pass through it and keep riding on the same road. One-half mile from the beginning of the campground find the first road junction and turn right. Ride a few yards to the next junction. Turn left and ride uphill following the sign to Scully Ridge (a right turn would have taken you into Water Canyon).

The ride toward Bobcat Ridge also connects to scully Ridge, and it is a long, steady climb. In 0.7 mile you climb over 200 feet to a junction in the road. Like the South Ridge Trail this path gains elevation quickly. Also, for lack of trees the views are wide open, giving a feeling of vastness at the ridge tops. On reaching the junction, turn right toward the high point of the ridge on Bobcat Ridge Trail. (Left is Scully Ridge Trail.)

When you reach the ridge a vast panorama unfolds. You find a deep, wide, completely primitive valley previously hidden from view — Brush Canyon. The name "Bobcat Ridge" refers to the many sightings of wildcats in this area. Not many people make it up to the high ridge. Too bad. A 360° view of the park plus two local mountain ranges await the rider willing to climb the heights of Bobcat Ridge.

Once you're on top of the ridge keep following the road around the right side of the valley. Elevation gains are about 400 feet in the space of 1.2 miles across the ridge above Brush Valley. At the far end of the valley a small saddle appears which is the exit from Bobcat Ridge and the park.

Beyond the park boundary, a road leads to a new housing tract. Eventually, when construction has been completed, the fences will fall and people will pass freely from the neighborhood into the park.

From the saddle at the end of Brush Canyon reverse directions for a long, fast downhill ride toward Aliso Valley. (At the saddle area there is also the beginning of a road down into Blue Mud Canyon. I have not ridden this road and cannot recommend it.) After leaving Bobcat Ridge follow the road to an intersection. Turn left. Continue downhill. At the next junction near the bottom of the hill turn right. In a few yards you make a quick left on the Aliso Canyon Road. From this last intersection you're only 0.5 mile from the campground. Follow the road, pass through the metal gate, and proceed through the camp area to the blacktop road. Turn left and begin your final ride to the ranch parking.

#5   Scully Ridge Loop
Length: 10.3 miles
Level of Difficulty: Intermediate
Elevation: Begin: 700+ feet. High point: 1,100 feet. End: 700+ feet

Leave the ranch parking lot heading south. Take the blacktop road to the campground and turn right. Ride through the camp, past the gate and beyond.

One-half mile from the beginning of the campground find the first road junction. Turn right and within a few yards turn left at the next junction and begin a long, steady climb up the ridge. In 0.7 mile another trail crosses. Take the left fork to Scully Ridge Trail (the right fork goes to Bobcat Ridge).

The Scully Ridge Trail is part old service road and new fire road. As a result, you can ride the full distance of the Western Ridge above Aliso Canyon. The road twists and turns back and forth across the ridgeline. Your views alternate between Brush Canyon and Aliso Canyon.

You pass another junction 1.5 miles farther south. (The left-hand trail from below is Brush Canyon Trail, which leads to Aliso Canyon. The right-hand trail drops below to the outer edge of Brush Canyon to a park entrance without public right-of-way.) Continue following Scully Ridge south along the ridge top. After 1 mile you'll notice another road approaching from below and to your left. This is the Scully Hill Trail from Aliso Valley.

Pass the Scully Hill Trail continuing south along the higher ridge for 0.4 mile where you'll find the descent to Santa Ana Canyon. In a half mile the trail drops almost 600 feet, just enough distance to have a lot of fun; it's a challenging and demanding ride! The final portion of this road turns to blacktop as you reach the bottom of Santa Ana Canyon.

Take a left, riding along the base of some steep hillsides. Soon, another dirt road forms and you follow it toward the north. The large meadow is private land but offers permission to pass. Continue on the dirt road that crosses the open area. You must open and close two stock gates gate when you're using this road. Horses often graze here and an open gate could mean lost animals. Please be careful to close and secure both gates.

Past the second gate, continue on the same trail a short distance until you come to a road crossing your path from the left. Turn left. This is the Aliso Canyon Road. Follow it to the metal gate (boundary). Cross through into the park and begin your 4-mile ride back to the ranch.

Later when you reach the posted junction with Water Canyon, turn right toward the campground. Make a left at the blacktop road when leaving the camp area. Your car is waiting just up the road.

#6   Raptor Ridge Loop
Length: 5.6 miles
Level of Difficulty: Intermediate
Elevation: Begin: 700+ feet. High point: 1,400+ feet. End: 700+ feet

As of mid-1992 there is only one single track trail open to mountain bikers in Chino Hills Park. It joins Raptor Ridge Trail and is part of this loop.

Exit the ranch parking area to the north. Pass in front of the ranger's residence, a yellow stucco house and continue north along the path. This portion of the park, an area of dead-end service roads, is less used and the roads are heavily overgrown. You're riding the northern portion of Aliso Valley Road. As you ride north of the ranch you'll see a ridgeline on the left that supports many electrical towers, Raptor Ridge.

One mile north of the ranch the road forks. Take the left fork, which climbs into the hills beneath a set of power lines. This is an unnamed single track. It passes through an area of higher hills and brush. Slowly and steadily it ascends the ridges at a sustainable pace. It's one of the best engineered trails I've ever ridden, cool to go up and better still to come down.

About 2.5 miles from the ranch you contour around a hill and find yourself on a road on Raptor Ridge. Turn right, riding to the end of the road. A small unnamed trail appears at road's end. Follow the trail out through the hills. Half a mile later you reach Telegraph Canyon Trail on the West Main Divide.

Turn left. Follow the road 0.4 mile through a saddle to East Main Divide where you now see a road intersecting from the left. Turn left and almost immediately you begin a steep power dive down a dirt road. This is the eastern part of Telegraph Canyon Trail. It travels parallel to Telegraph Canyon back toward the ranger station. The road finally levels out slightly but it's fast all the way to the end. Caution is necessary on this tough downhill ride. Before you can tell yourself what a good time you're having, you come to the end of the trail and the crossroads to the ranch area where you turn left onto the blacktop road. The parking area is just a few yards ahead.

Variations: The downhill ride on the unnamed portion of Raptor Ridge Trail is one of my favorite rides in the park. It's moderately technical and also quick. The ride description above has you going up this section. To do it downhill, take either the eastern part of Telegraph Canyon Trail or South Ridge Trail to the West Main Divide. Turn right off Telegraph Canyon Trail onto the unnamed footpath and begin your ride. South Ridge Trail—with a gentler ascent—joins Telegraph Canyon Trail about 1/2 mile east of this junction.

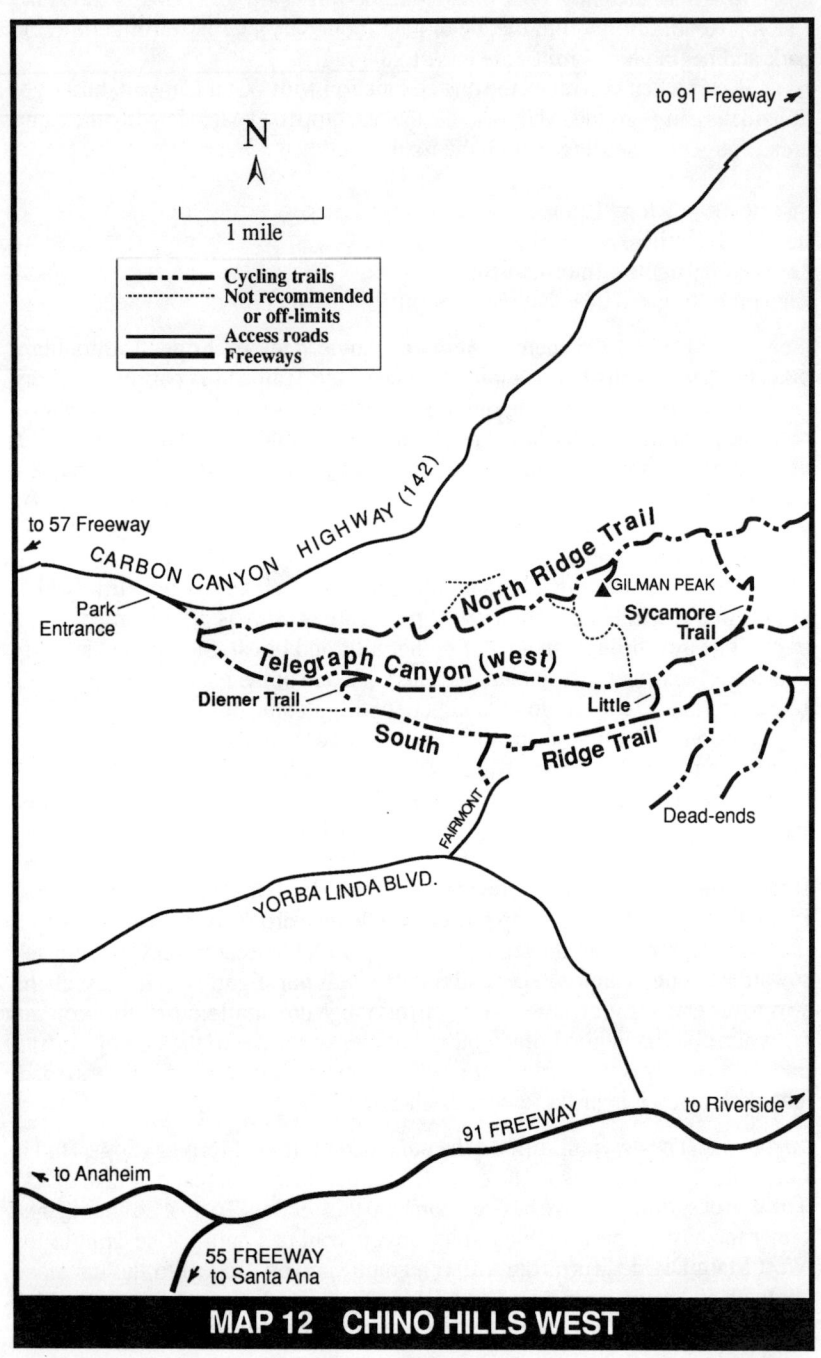

N

1 mile

Legend	
—··—··—	Cycling trails
··············	Not recommended or off-limits
———	Access roads
▬▬▬	Freeways

to 91 Freeway ↗

to 57 Freeway ↙

CARBON CANYON HIGHWAY (142)

Park Entrance

North Ridge Trail

▲ GILMAN PEAK

Sycamore Trail

Telegraph Canyon (west)

Diemer Trail

Little

South Ridge Trail

Dead-ends

FAIRMONT

YORBA LINDA BLVD.

91 FREEWAY

to Riverside ↗

↙ to Anaheim

55 FREEWAY
to Santa Ana ↙

MAP 12   CHINO HILLS WEST

CHAPTER 15

CHINO HILLS STATE PARK: WEST ENTRY, CROSS-PARK RIDES AND SOUTH RIDGE ENTRIES

Getting There: In the Brea area of Orange County traveling on the 57 Freeway, exit at Lambert. Drive east until the street becomes Brea Canyon Drive. After 2.2 miles you'll see Carbon Canyon Regional Park on your right.

Carbon Canyon Regional Park is the best place to park for your trip into the western Chino Hills. It's patrolled, cheap, and easy to get in and out of (just bring two crisp Yankee Dollars to feed the "android" lot attendant).

Topo Maps: Orange County topo or USGS 7.5 minute series (Yorba Linda, Prado Dam)

#1   Telegraph Canyon Trail to the Main Divide
Length: 11 miles round trip
Water: Carbon Canyon Park
Level of Difficulty: Beginner, intermediate
Elevation: Begin: 500+ feet. High point: 1,500+ feet. End: 500+ feet.

Leave Carbon Canyon Park at the entry way and turn right, riding past an orchard. At a metal gate pass around and onto a blacktop road. The road dips into a creek bed. Most of the time there's water running in the creek; quite a bit in wintertime. The creek has a firm bottom so don't be afraid to roll on through. You rise out of the creek bed onto the other side and come upon another fence. Note the open entry and pass through. At this point you'll see one dirt road going right and another left. Take the right-hand road. The left road climbs into the hills to become the North Ridge Trail.

Continue on the right-hand trail a few yards until you see another dirt road breaking off to the left near some park displays. Turn left and begin the Telegraph Canyon Trail (West).

Telegraph Canyon Trail begins as a very narrow valley following the bed of a seasonal creek. The canyon widens as it twists its way deeper into the hills. At first, the canyon is largely grasslands with a few scattered bushes and trees. This later gives way to larger stands of oak and huge sycamore trees that dominate the landscape. The entire ride through Telegraph Canyon has a nearly imperceptible elevation gain. In 5.5 miles you climb approximately 1,000 feet but hardly notice it due to its gradual nature.

There are many trails leading out of Telegraph Valley to the other locations within the park. As you pedal up the valley road, you will see the following connector trails:

Diemer Trail (names after the treatment plant up the hill on the right) leads from Telegraph Valley to the top of South Ridge. It begins on your right 1.5 miles from Carbon Canyon parking lot, and it climbs steeply up South Ridge. *Little Canyon Trail,* 1.8 miles beyond Diemer Trail, drops steeply from the South Ridge connecting with Telegraph Canyon. Continue past this road. *Sycamore Trail* intersects Telegraph Canyon Trail from the left 1/2 mile beyond Little Canyon Trail. From the North Ridge it drops almost 500 feet from the top of the ridge in a very short distance, making it a downhill to remember. *McDermont Trail* comes in from the left 1/2 mile beyond Sycamore Trail. It leads up to the top of North Ridge and represents the very end of the North Ridge Trail. A few hundred yards beyond McDermont Trail you'll find a crossroads of trails leading to various areas of the park. This is the Main Divide area.

On Telegraph Canyon Trail, several hundred yards east of McDermont Trail, you enter the Main Divide (West). What is the Main Divide? It is a north-south ridge, approximately 1,500 feet at its high point, that roughly separates the east and west sides of Chino Hills State Park, which is primarily comprised of are ridges and valleys running roughly east and west.

Find a dirt road off to your left (a dead-end). Next to the dead-end is a small footpath also on your left. (This is the unnamed single track attached to Raptor Ridge described in Ride #5, Chapter 14.) Continue riding on Telegraph Canyon Trail past the footpath around a bend and over the crest of the Divide. You are now on the East Main Divide.

A short distance after passing over the Divide you'll see a trail on the left heading quickly downhill. This is the Telegraph Canyon Trail (East), which empties into Aliso Valley. Continuing on the Telegraph Trail, a few hundred yards after the last connection, see three trailheads on your right. The left road is a dead-end. The right, going downhill, is the South Ridge Trail and a *wild* ride to Aliso Valley below. The right path going uphill is the South Ridge Trail heading back (west) toward the Telegraph Canyon entrance to the park. This junction marks the end of Telegraph Canyon Trail (West). To return to your car simply reverse the previous directions.

#2 North Ridge Trail Loop
Length: 9.6 miles or 12 miles
Water: Carbon Canyon Park
Level of Difficulty: Intermediate
Elevation: Begin: 500 feet. High point: 1,600+ feet. End: 1,200+ feet.

Exit Carbon Canyon Park and turn right. Ride past the orchard and around the metal gate onto a blacktop road. The road will dip shortly into a creek bed. Don't be afraid to pedal through to the other side. Once up over the creek bed note a wire fence in front of you with a gate. Pass through and you'll find two paths. One goes right (Telegraph Canyon) and the other goes left up a ridge. Take the left road and soon you'll be high onto the North Ridge.

This path runs above and parallel with Telegraph Canyon. The trail crisscrosses back and forth over the ridgeline. The area has many trees, but is primarily grassland. It's a great, wide open place with occasional views of snow-capped mountains. The neighboring hills and valleys are tranquil and beautiful. Reminders of the area's ranching past appear as fences, corral posts, and the like.

The trail up the North Ridge is well built. The climb up the hill is relentless but not unreasonable due to the quality of the road. You'll see 1.3 miles from the trail's beginning the first connector road intersecting your path from the left. This path leads to Soquel Canyon. (Hikers only—none of the roads from Soquel Canyon to North Ridge Trail may be used by cyclists.)

Continuing east, you pass two hiking trails on the right before reaching a dirt road that heads right to Gilman Peak (2 miles beyond the Soquel Trail). This is a side trip worth taking. It's a short ride up, and at 1,685 feet Gilman is the second tallest mountain in Chino Hills State Park. You have beautiful scenery and a view to the San Gabriel Mountains.

One-half mile from the peak see another trail intersecting yours from the left. This is another road onto private land below in Soquel Canyon. Pass by. A few hundred yards beyond this last trail another road appears on your right. This is Sycamore Trail leading to Telegraph Canyon below. In 0.7 miles the trail drops approximately 500 feet. This is a fast and challenging ride, the most popular exit from the North Ridge Trail.

From Sycamore Trail you may elect to continue east (toward the Main Divide) on the North Ridge Trail. From the Sycamore Trail junction, the remainder of North Ridge Trail is sandy, rocky, and generally disagreeable. This section isn't ridden a lot so it's a very private place to be if you enjoy that.

In another 1.3 miles the trail dead-ends into private ranch land. To reach Telegraph Canyon below retrace your ride back a few hundred yards to a wide road going downhill. Make a left and follow the track a few hundred yards. The road will fork. Go right down McDermont Trail to reach Telegraph Canyon Trail (left fork dead-ends into a hiking trail). This road is in good condition with few people ever on it. It's wide open and very fast to Telegraph Canyon below. On reaching the canyon road turn right (west) and begin the return to your car.

#3   South Ridge Trail - Main Divide Loop

Length: 14.5 miles
Water: Carbon Canyon Park
Level of Difficulty: Intermediate
Elevation: Begin: 400+ feet. High point: 1,700+ feet. End: 400+ feet.

Like the other trails of the West Park entrance leave your car at Carbon Canyon Park. Turn right from the parking lot, ride past the orchard, go trough the gate and the small creek. After the creek is a fence with an open area to cross through. On the other side of the fence turn right. Take this right fork a short distance until a dirt road intersects your path from the left. Turn left and enter Telegraph Canyon.

At this point the canyon is very narrow. It is grassland with a few small trees hugging the shores of Telegraph Canyon Creek. 1.2 miles up Telegraph Canyon note a dirt road joining the main road from the right. This road is Diemer Trail, the first connector to South Ridge Trail. It is a short but steep climb to the top of the ridge.

Once on top the views of Orange County are magnificent. All of North

County lies at your feet and in the distance see the coast and skyscrapers of Newport Beach. The South Ridge is a wide, high, grassy place with little to block the outstanding views of the surrounding area.

On the ridge you begin a long, gradual climb to the east. For the next 2 miles of this ride there are several roads coming up from the right. All these roads lead onto private land and are not legally usable. After 2 miles, however, there are several legal entries onto South Ridge, which are discussed at the end of this chapter.

In the first 2 miles of South Ridge Trail you'll note that several housing developments have been built up to the borders of the park. After that, however, all development drops off into the distance. The hills become higher and the area more remote behind a series of steep canyons and ridges. On this portion of South Ridge Trail there are few trees, only vast grassy slopes exaggerating a sense of distance and isolation. Cattle are occasionally allowed to graze here and I've seen herds of 8 to 10 deer running across the hills.

A road appears from the left 2.2 miles east of the Diemer Trail entry onto South Ridge Trail. This is Little Canyon Trail linking up with Telegraph Canyon. It's a steep, fast drop (more like a power dive than a bike ride). You can shorten your trip here by linking up with Telegraph Canyon Trail below and returning to your car.

Continue east along the ridge and gain more elevation. Several more roads appear on the left, but they're dead-end utility roads. Two and a half miles from Little Canyon Trail you reach San Juan Hill. At 1,783 feet this is the highest spot in the park. A series of power lines/electrical towers cross the flank of the hill (an unmistakable landmark).

At the base of San Juan Hill lies a crossroads. Continue straight and the ridge begins dropping. You're now directly above the Main Divide. The turnoff for Telegraph Canyon Road is 0.8 miles below the San Juan Hill crossroads. Turn left, crossing the Main Divide and down into Telegraph Canyon. The return to your car is a long, pleasant downhill glide.

Note: Few people travel here so you're likely to see no one if you explore the area. The views are fantastic. At the San Juan Hill crossroads, turn south (right) away from the main park. In a few hundred yards pass by a dead-end road coming in from the right. There is a fork about 3/4 mile farther. Taking either one is okay; they are parallel roads, separated by a narrow canyon, and both end at private property. Retrace your steps to San Juan Hill to return to your vehicle.

Cross Park Rides

There are several cross-park rides involving car shuttles. One car is parked at Carbon Canyon Park (see Ride #1, this chapter) and another at the Chino Hills Park Headquarters (see Ride #1, Chapter 14). When positioning cars, Highway 142 through Carbon Canyon is your most direct auto link between the two ends of the park.

To go from Carbon Canyon Park to the west side of Chino Hills, turn right out of the parking lot and drive east on Carbon Canyon Highway (142).

This becomes Chino Hills Parkway after 7.5 miles and leads to Highway 71. Go south on 71 to Central Avenue exit. Make a right and then a quick left onto Pomona-Rincon Road. Drive south 0.4 mile to Soquel Canyon Parkway and turn right, continuing on to the park entrance as described in Chapter 14.

To reach the west side of the park from the east side, go to the corner of Soquel Canyon and Pomona-Rincon and turn left. Drive a short distance to Central Avenue to cross Highway 71, then turn left quickly on Highway 71. Go north and turn left onto Chino Hills Parkway. Continue driving east as it become Carbon Canyon Parkway and reaches Carbon Canyon Park. Time to ride!

#4   Telegraph Canyon Trail to Carbon Canyon Park
Length: 7.8 miles
Level of Difficulty: Intermediate
Elevation: Begin: 700+ feet. High point: 1,400+ feet. End: 400+ feet.

From the ranch parking area in the west park, take your bike south to the stop sign. Turn right on the dirt road going uphill. This is Telegraph Canyon Trail (eastern half). Begin a steady uphill ride. The last section of this road becomes very steep. One mile from the parking lot a road appears from the right, connecting with Raptor Ridge. Ignore it.

A mile later you come to a crossroads. Turn right. Follow the road through a small saddle and onto the West Main Divide. You are now on Telegraph Canyon Road (West) headed toward your car. On the right side you will pass a well-worn footpath (unnamed, see previous ride), as well as a dead-end road just a few feet away from the single track. Ignore both paths.

You are now on a portion of Telegraph Canyon Road that is heavily wooded and shady. The road drops steadily and you have a long glide back to the mouth of Telegraph Canyon. Exit the canyon and head out toward your second vehicle.

#5   South Ridge & Telegraph Canyon Trails to Carbon Canyon Park
Length: 8.6 miles
Level of Difficulty: Intermediate
Elevation: Begin: 700 feet. High point: 1,700+ feet. End: 400+ feet.

The bad news about South Ridge Trail is the steep climb from the eastern part of the park. The good news is the next 5 miles of downhill coasting from San Juan Hill to Telegraph Canyon. The trip goes very fast from that point.

Begin in the west park and roll your bike south from the ranch parking area to the South Ridge Trail. It climbs nearly a thousand feet from the ranch to San Juan Hill in 2.3 miles, and you need to keep a good, steady pace for this hill climb. Your rewards: panoramic views of the park and surrounding ridges.

From here on, go straight, ignoring every other intersecting trail along the way except one: turn right on Diemer Trail, which comes in 6.4 miles from the ranch the trail. Descend into Telegraph Canyon. Turn left and ride west until you exit the canyon and return to your car.

#6   Telegraph Canyon / Raptor Ridge via Unnamed Single Track
Length: 8.5 miles
Level of Difficulty: Intermediate
Elevation: Begin: 400+ feet. High point: 1,400+ feet. End: 700+ feet.

From Carbon Canyon Park head to Telegraph Canyon Trail as described
in Ride #1. Turn left. You enter the narrow canyon past some park billboards.
As you ride east, the valley opens a little wider and, as the elevations get higher,
you see many changes in vegetation from grasses to forests. Follow Telegraph
Canyon 5.5 miles to the West Main Divide. About 1/2 mile east of McDermont
Trail, pass a dead-end road on the left and then take a left on the nearby footpath.
This is the unnamed single track section that heads to Raptor Ridge. The narrow
path heads through the high brush and grass off across the ridges. Soon it crests
the Main Divide and begins losing elevation on the other side—a high-speed
roller coaster headed for Aliso Valley. Caution required. Fun is unavoidable.

Half a mile from the crossroads with Telegraph Canyon the trail connects
with the main road on Raptor Ridge. In a few yards look for a footpath entering
the road from the left. Take a hard left onto the path and bounce back up into
the brush and hills without losing a step. Keep going down the path toward the
valley below. At last, as you pass beneath some power lines, you see a
crossroads a little way ahead. Turn right on the road. In 1 mile you will ride into
the ranch area and connect with your second car.

South Ridge Entries

There are several entries onto the South Ridge Trail from Yorba Linda city
streets. From the 57 Freeway (near California State Fullerton) exit on Yorba
Linda Boulevard heading east. After several miles turn left on Fairmont and
drive into the hills. All these entries are found on streets just off Fairmont.

Blue Gum: Take Fairmont (north) to Rim Crest. Turn left. Follow to the
corner of Blue Gum and Rim Crest. There's a small dirt road/parking area at the
corner. Walk down into the dirt road area and you'll see the entry to the park.

Quail Circle: Take Fairmont north (past Rim Crest) to Quail Circle Park
on a side street. You'll see a horse trail leaving the street area up into the hills.
Take it to the top of South Ridge.

Rim Road Terrace: Take Fairmont north past Quail Circle to Condor
Ridge. Turn left on Condor Ridge and continue to the street's dead-end. This is
your entry point, a fire road kept open to the top of South Ridge Trail. It's very
steep but a short distance to the top.

Casino Ridge: Drive north on Fairmont to its dead-end into San Antonio
Road. Turn right on San Antonio. Drive downhill a short distance to Casino
Ridge. Turn left on Casino Ridge into a small cul-de-sac. A dirt road fire road
heads up onto South Ridge Trail. You reach South Ridge Trail after 1.5 miles
and 800 feet of elevation gain. You are 1 mile west of San Juan Hill.

—APPENDIX—

First Aid – *by Réanne Douglass*

Several years ago on a mountain biking trip, I miscalculated a sharp turn on a sandy stretch of dirt road, went flying and turned my right shin into raw meat. I didn't have a first aid kit with me. Why bother? After all, I was cycling off-road, no traffic around, and I planned to be gone just part of the day. When I got home, I took a shower, cleaned my wound and applied some antibiotic cream. Three days later, Don had to carry me to the doctor. A staph infection – that took three pain-filled weeks to control – had set in. *Don't be careless like I was.* Carry and use a First Aid Kit. You can purchase one at bike shops or sporting goods stores, or you can make your own. For day rides, we suggest the following items:

8 Bandaids 1" x 3"	8 Aspirin Tablets or Aspirin Substitute
6 Antiseptic Swabs or	8 Gauze Pads 3" x 3"
1 oz. Hydrogen Peroxide	4 Antacid Tablets
1 Roll Adhesive Tape	1 Elastic Bandage
1 Moleskin 3" x 4"	1 Needle
1 Single-Edge Razor Blade	Waterproof Matches (in film can)
Sunscreen 15 SPF or more	Prescription Medicine (if applicable)

IMBA Rules of the Trail

1. **Ride on open trails only.** Respect trail and road closures (ask if not sure), avoid possible trespass on private land, obtain permits and authorization as may be required. Federal and State wilderness areas are closed to cycling.

2. **Leave no trace.** Be sensitive to the dirt beneath you. Even on open trails, you should not ride under conditions where you will leave evidence of your passing, such as on certain soils shortly after a rain. Observe the different types of soils and trail construction; practice low-impact cycling. This also means staying on the trail and not creating any new ones. Be sure to pack out at least as much as you pack in.

3. **Control your bicycle!** Inattention for even a second can cause disaster. Excessive speed maims and threatens people; there is no excuse for it!

4. **Always yield trail.** Make known your approach well in advance. A friendly greeting (or bell) is considerate and works well; startling someone may cause loss of trail access. Show your respect when passing others by slowing to a walk or even stopping. Anticipate that other trail users may be around corners or in blind spots.

5. **Never spook animals.** All animals are startled by an unannounced approach, a sudden movement, or a loud noise. This can be dangerous for you, others, and the animals. Give animals extra room and time to adjust to you. In passing, use special care and follow the directions of horseback riders (ask if uncertain). Running cattle and disturbing wild animals is a serious offense. Leave gates as you found them, or as marked.

6. **Plan ahead.** Know your equipment, your ability, and the area in which you are riding – and prepare accordingly. Be self-sufficient at all times, wear a helmet, keep your machine in good repair, and carry necessary supplies for changes in weather or other conditions. A well-executed trip is satisfying to you and not a burden or offense to others.

Outdoor Books and Maps from Fine Edge Productions

Mountain Biking the High Sierra

Guide 1	Owens Valley and Inyo County, Second Edition	$8.95
Guide 2	Mammoth Lakes and Mono County, Third Edition	$8.95
Guide 3A	Lake Tahoe South, Second Edition	$8.95
Guide 3B	Lake Tahoe North, Second Edition	$8.95

Mountain Biking the Coast Range

Guide 4	Ventura County and the Sespe, New Third Edition	$8.95
Guide 5	Santa Barbara County, Third Edition	$8.95
Guide 7	Santa Monica Mountains, New Second Edition	$8.95
Guide 8	Saugus District of the Angeles N.F. with Mt. Pinos	$8.95
Guide 9	San Gabriel Mountains, Angeles N.F.	$8.95
Guide 10	San Bernardino Mountains	$8.95
	Includes Lytle Creek & San Jacinto (6/93)	
Guide 11	Orange County and Cleveland National Forest	$8.95
	Includes Santa Ana Mountains & Chino Hills	

Mountain Biking Maps (topographical)

Santa Ana Mountains, Orange County, Cleveland National Forest – Map, with trail profiles & descriptions (6/93)	$8.95
San Gabriel Mountains – West Map, w/profiles & trail descriptions Angeles National Forest and Verdugo Mountains	$8.95
Santa Monica Mountains – Map, w/ profiles & trail descriptions	$8.95
Mammoth Mountain, Mono Lake High Sierra – Map w/ profiles & trail desc.	$8.95
North Lake Tahoe Basin Recreation Map, w/profiles & trail descriptions	$8.95
South Lake Tahoe Basin Recreation Map, w/profiles & trail descriptions	$8.95
Excelsior District, Tahoe N.F., Lake Tahoe Region, Hwy. 80	$6.95
Crystal Basin, Eldorado N.F., Lake Tahoe Region, Hwy. 50	$6.95
Moab, Utah, Slick Rock	$5.95

Also available:

Favorite Pedal Tours of Northern California	$12.95
44 classic rides originally published in California Bicyclist	
Ski Touring the Eastern High Sierra	$8.95
Beginning and Intermediate Cross-Country Day Trips	
Exploring California's Channel Islands, an Artist's View	$6.95

Additional books and maps in process; manuscripts are solicited.

For current titles and prices, please send SASE.

To order any of these items see your local dealer or order direct.
Please include $2.00 for shipping. California residents add sales tax.
20% discount on orders of 5 or more items.

Fine Edge Productions, Route 2, Box 303, Bishop, California 93514